THE ROCKY HORROR SHOW BOOK

THE ROCKY HORROR SHOW BOOK

JAMES HARDING

SIDGWICK & JACKSON
LONDON

. . . and Richard created

SOME OF THE AUDIENCE AT A ROCKY HORROR SHOW PERFORMANCE

ROCKY

on such a night...1986

On a dark stormy night in the melancholy suburbs of south-east London the *Rocky Horror Show* touring company was playing the Lewisham Theatre. Rain spat down the streets and harried passers-by. If, outside, everything was chilly and dark, within the theatre all was exuberance and glittering lasers. The Narrator delivered his unctuous phrases to a barrage of cheerful obscenity from the audience. When Brad and Janet lurched through the storm umbrellas snapped open and waved jubilantly. As the couple started to sing 'There's a light over at the Frankenstein place' candles flared and glimmered eerily throughout the auditorium. Frank whisked Rocky off to the wedding chamber in a shower of confetti hurled from the stalls. His announcement of a banquet was greeted with a hail of Kit-Kat bars that clattered around him on the stage. He picked one up and tried to put it into his codpiece for future reference. 'H'm,' he murmured, 'not enough room.'

At the end, when the company reprised all the main numbers, the audience could restrain themselves no more. They danced along the rows of seats and down the aisles.

Immediately beneath the stage an ecstatic crowd rocked and stamped in time to the music. Among them were look-alike Franks, Riff-Raffs and Magentas. In a brief silence Frank addressed them. 'Thank you for coming,' he leered. They shrieked with lubricious laughter. 'We're doing it again tonight,' he added, 'and twice tomorrow night!' They roared once more. Many of them had not been born when *The Rocky Horror Show* was first performed. Quite a few of them had been babes in arms. During the interval they thronged the foyer eagerly snapping up *Rocky Horror* T-shirts, souvenir programmes, badges and photographs. What is the secret of *Rocky*'s enduring appeal? Why should each new generation seize on it with the same enthusiasm it evoked when it first appeared? Everywhere in the world, it seems, there is, at any given moment, a performance of *The Rocky Horror Show* going on. It takes serious matters lightly and light matters seriously. It pounds non-stop at the audience, jeers, laughs, mocks, gives them no time to think before plunging into the next outrageous song. *Rocky* defies the years. It is always young and always fresh. How did it all begin?

on such a night...1973

On a dark stormy night in Sloane Square The Theatre Upstairs was featuring a new production called *The Rocky Horror Show*. Although it was 16 June thunder rolled across a lurid sky, lightning crackled and rain swept the streets in torrents. Housed in the Royal Court, The Theatre Upstairs specialized in off-beat try-outs and derived its name from the fact that to reach it you climb three flights. It had room for an audience of sixty-three people.

Those who mounted the stairs on that unseasonable June night might have thought they were going to the theatre. They found themselves, instead, confronted with a run-down seedy cinema. Hunch-backed ghouls and ushers wearing oddly fixed grins — later you realized they were masks — showed them to rows of sagging red seats. Up on the stage a dusty old cinema screen lolled drunkenly. A large placard announced: 'The Sloane Cinema regrets the inconvenience caused to patrons during renovations. Modern 3-screen cinema will open shortly.'

As the spectators wedged themselves into their seats they glanced at duplicated typed programmes thrust ungraciously into their hands by the sinister ushers. Tim Curry, they read, played Dr Frank'n'Furter. Julie Covington was Janet Weiss and Patricia Quinn acted both the Usherette and Magenta. Little Nell was Columbia and Jonathan Adams the Narrator. Paddie O'Hagan doubled as Eddie and Dr Everett Scott. Rayner Bourton was Rocky Horror and Christopher Malcolm Brad Majors. The part of Riff-Raff was taken by Richard O'Brien who had written not only the play but also the music and lyrics.

The programme went on to record the company's gratitude to Coca-Cola for the loan of a Coca-Cola machine and to Lyons

PROGRAMME COVER FOR THE ORIGINAL *ROCKY HORROR SHOW* PRODUCTION

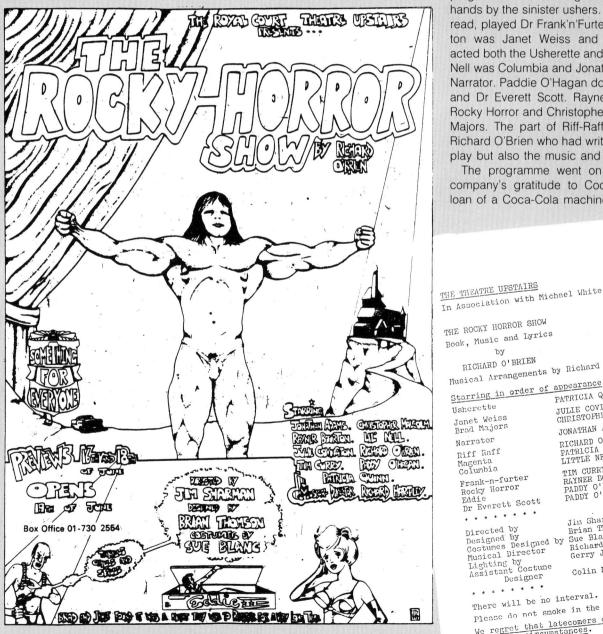

THE THEATRE UPSTAIRS
In Association with Michael White

THE ROCKY HORROR SHOW
Book, Music and Lyrics
by
RICHARD O'BRIEN
Musical Arrangements by Richard Hartley

Starring in order of appearance:

Usherette	PATRICIA QUINN
Janet Weiss	JULIE COVINGTON
Brad Majors	CHRISTOPHER MALCOLM
Narrator	JONATHAN ADAMS
Riff Raff	RICHARD O'BRIEN
Magenta	PATRICIA QUINN
Columbia	LITTLE NELL
Frank-n-furter	TIM CURRY
Rocky Horror	RAYNER BOURTON
Eddie	PADDY O'HAGAN
Dr Everett Scott	PADDY O'HAGAN

* * * * * * * *

Directed by	Jim Sharman
Designed by	Brian Thomson
Costumes Designed by	Sue Blane
Musical Director	Richard (Ritz) Hartley
Lighting by	Gerry Jenkinson
Assistant Costume Designer	Colin MacNeil

* * * * * * * *

There will be no interval.
Please do not smoke in the theatre.
We regret that latecomers cannot be admitted under any circumstances.

Maid for the use of a refreshment tray. A more ominous undertone emerged in a reference to the Hammersmith Medical School which lent surgical gowns, gloves and masks, and to St Mary's Hospital for hospital equipment. The acknowledgements offered 'special thanks to Hammer Films without whom . . .' This remark must have enchanted the actor Vincent Price who figured among the first-night audience with his wife Coral Browne. Was he not the saturnine villain of many horror films based on Edgar Allan Poe stories? Was he not, in person, the Abominable Dr Phibes?

At 10.30 p.m. all but three of the ghostly ushers melted away into the darkness. These three, whose masks concealed the faces of Riff-Raff, Columbia and Eddie, moved through the audience and up to the stage where an usherette sat on a box. She was draped in white gauze, her face illuminated only by the light from her ice-cream tray. The three ushers crept over the 'Odeon' carpet and chorussed: 'Glad you could come tonight.' They pulled the gauze away and a spot lit her up.

ayed by:
ı Blair

ve Channing

ırtin Fitzgibbon
ıchard Hartley

Electric/Accoustic
Guitar
Bass Guitar
Alto/Tenor Sax
Bass Guitar
Drums
Piano/Organ
Synthesiser

* * * * * * *

tage Manager
assistant Stage Managers)

Chris Peachment
Alkis Kritikos
Marion Kernahan
Peter Hunt

Lighting Operator
* * * * * * *

Grateful thanks to:
Andrews Hair Artist for Men for hair spray; Britax London Ltd. for the loan of seat belts; Coca Cola for the coca cola machine; Peter Cox Ltd. for lending many tarpaulins; the Glasgow Citizens' Theatre for supplying additional costumes and Mr S Loizou of the Hammersmith Medical School for surgical gowns, gloves and masks. Bill Lewington supplied the cymbals and Lyons Maid lent us the refreshments tray: our thanks also to St Mary's Hospital, Paddington for the loan of the hospital equipment, the Sander Mirror Co. who gave us a lot of mirrors. Peter Jones kindly lent us the mirror on wheels and special thanks to Hammer Films without whom . . . .

* * * * * * *

THE THEATRE UPSTAIRS

Director
Manager
Secretary

Box Office – 01 730 2554

Nicholas Wright
Harriet Cruickshank
Secretary

◄ INSIDE SPREAD OF THE ORIGINAL
PROGRAMME

PAT QUINN AS THE USHERETTE (1973
PRODUCTION)

science fiction – wah, wah, wah

A synthesizer twanged mournfully and she sang:

> Michael Rennie was ill
> The day the earth stood still
> But he told us where we stand
> And Flash Gordon was there
> In silver underwear
> Claude Rains was the invisible man
> Then something went wrong
> For Fay Wray and King Kong
> They got caught in a celluloid jam
> Then at a deadly pace
> It came from outer space
> And this is how the message ran.
> 'Science fiction – ('Wah, wah, wah',
>   sang the ushers),
> 'Double feature ('Doh, doh, doh')
> 'Dr X ('Oo, oo, oo')
> '– will build a creature
> 'See androids fighting – ('Oo, oo, oo')
> '– Brad & Janet
> 'Anne Francis stars in – ('Oo, oo, oo')
> 'Forbidden Planet ('Oh, oh, oh')
> 'Oh, at the late-night double feature
> 'Picture show.'

The sound of wedding bells was heard. Brad and Janet, 'two young ordinary healthy kids', emerged from attending the wedding of one of their college friends. Wasn't it wonderful, breathed Janet, and wasn't the bride radiantly beautiful? But Brad has something more to say:

> The future is ours so let's plan it ('Janet'
>   chorus the ushers)
> So please don't tell me to can it
>   ('Janet')
> I've one thing to say and that's . . .
> Damn it – Janet – I love you.

He gives her an engagement ring and she squeals:

> Now we're engaged and I'm so glad
>   ('Oh Brad')
> That you've met Mom and you know
>   Dad ('Oh Brad')
> I've one thing to say and that's . . .
> Brad – I'm mad – for you too.

They decide they will go and tell the good news to Dr Everett Scott, the science teacher in whose college class they first met. While they drive away in Brad's car a smooth and velvet-voiced Narrator takes up the story. 'I would like,' he says, fumbling with a large dusty tome, ' – if I may – to take you on a strange journey.' It seemed a fairly ordinary night, he continues, when Brad and Janet set off to visit their old teacher. But dark clouds were gathering and a storm was on the way. 'It was a night out,' he concludes, 'they were to remember for a very – long – time.'

The storm breaks, a tyre is punctured and Brad and Janet come to a stop in desolate countryside. What do they do next? 'Didn't we pass a castle back down the road a few miles? Maybe they have a telephone I might use,' says Brad resourcefully.

They both get out and walk through the blinding rain until they see a light in the distance. Janet chirrups:

> In the velvet darkness
> Of the blackest night
> Burning bright – there's a guiding star
> No matter what or who you are.
> There's a light
> Over at the Frankenstein place.

Whereupon the gaunt face of Riff-Raff appears in unholy light to join in the chorus. Brad rings the doorbell. After a lengthy pause Riff-Raff peers out as if looking for someone else. He responds to Brad's effusive explanations with a laconic: 'You're wet.' Reluctantly, as lightning flashes, he admits them to the castle.

The Narrator materializes. 'And so, after braving the inclement weather, and some not too little time – it seemed that fortune had smiled on Brad and Janet and that they had found the assistance that their plight required,' he observes.
'Or had they?'

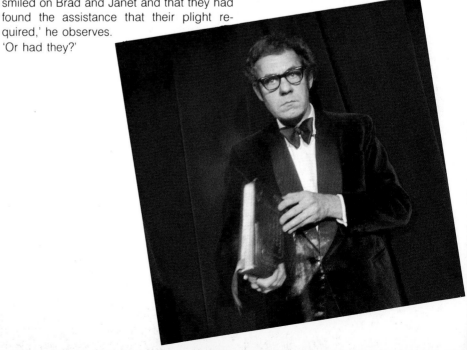

JULIE COVINGTON (JANET) AND
CHRISTOPHER MALCOLM (BRAD)
AS JANET AND BRAD ▶

JONATHAN ADAMS AS THE
NARRATOR (1973)

• • •

While they dry their wet clothes they are startled by the entry of Riff-Raff accompanied by Magenta the Domestic and Columbia the Groupie. Even more unnerving is the sudden apparition of Dr Frank'n'Furter himself, a glamorous fishnet-and-black-suspendered Supertart. 'Master!' cry Riff-Raff and the girls. Frank introduces himself.

> Don't get strung out by the way that I
>   look
> Don't judge a book by its cover
> I'm not much of a man
> By the light of day
> But by night I'm one hell of a lover
> I'm just a sweet transvestite
> From Transexual
> Transylvania.

RICHARD O'BRIEN (RIFF-RAFF), JONATHAN ADAMS (NARRATOR), AND PAT QUINN (MAGENTA) (1973 PRODUCTION)

Then, with the collusion of the Narrator who so far forgets his dignity as to show off the steps, they all dance the 'Time Warp':

> It's astounding — time is fleeting
> Madness takes its toll
> But listen closely — not for very much
>   longer
> I've got to keep control.
> I remember doing the time warp
> Drinking those moments when
> The blackness would hit me — and the
>   void would be calling
> Let's do the time warp again
> Let's do the time warp again.
> It's just a jump to the left
> And then a step to the right
> With your hands on your hips
> You bring your knees in tight
> But it's the pelvic thrust
> That really drives you insane
> Let's do the time warp again
> Let's do the time warp again.

RAYNER BOURTON (ROCKY) AND TIM CURRY (FRANK)

At Frank's arrival the show has moved into top gear. He creates his monster, as did Mary Shelley's scientist, amid much flashing of coloured lights and gurgling of test tubes. His creation, though, is not at all monstrous but turns out to be a gorgeous hunk of a man christened Rocky, golden-haired and gold-spangled in golden briefs. (One of Frank's more unsuccessful earlier attempts, Eddie the delivery boy, has to be liquidated and stuffed back into the Coke machine.) Brad and Janet, that fine upstanding young couple, undergo adventures such as they had never dreamed of in their worst nightmares. They are reunited, at last, with their old teacher Dr Scott, but under circumstances which force them, and him, to dance in a chorus line wearing suspender-belts and black stockings of the sort paraded by Frank. 'Don't dream it — be it,' Frank croons to them as they collapse around him into a swirling mass of arms and legs and heads. He dies, as does Rocky, struck down by a death ray from Riff-Raff's laser gun. 'They didn't like me!' screams Riff-Raff. 'They never liked me.' He activates the transit crystal and, with Magenta, zooms back to the planet of Transexual in the galaxy of Transylvania. A meditative reprise of 'Science Fiction, Double Feature' brings to an end ninety minutes of concentrated action which had invoked murder, cannibalism, rape, sodomy, fellatio, transvestism and cunnilingus. Discerning observers also claim to have detected incest.

LET'S DO, THE.....

TIME WARP

BASIC STEPS

3,4,5.
L R
← 1
L R
START
3,4,5.
R
2

1 (ITS JUST A) JUMP TO THE LEFT, WITH HANDS UP
2 A STEP TO THE RIGHT (TIME-WARPER ANNETTE FUNICELLO SUGGESTS A VERY WIDE STEP.)
3* (WITH YOUR HANDS ON YOUR HIPS) YOU BRING YOUR KNEES IN TIGHT.
4 (THEN) THE PELVIC THRUST (IF REPEATED FIVE TIMES, IT NEARLY DRIVES YOU INSA-A-ANE)
5 HIPSWIVEL (IF NOT DRIVEN INSA-A-ANE BY STEP FOUR)
6 LET'S DO THE TIME WARP AGAIN!!
* THOSE WITH LIMB DISABILITIES MAY FIND IT NECESSARY TO ALTER OR DELETE THIS ACTION, BUT NO EXCUSES FOR ALTERATIONS TO STEPS FOUR AND FIVE.

AS FEATURED IN THE ROCKY HORROR SHOW!

17   11

an acid bon-bon

The first-night audience on that rainy June evening loved *The Rocky Horror Show*. The swift-paced action gave them no time to think. Members of the cast swung down over them from a gantry up in the ceiling, rushed along catwalks and flew down ramps. The novel spoof of horror movies and sci-fi epics wrapped up in a pounding restless rock beat left them breathless. Perhaps, mostly, it was the lightning humour, the camp but loving irreverence with which it sent up Hollywood B-movies, that delighted them.

Next morning and in the days that followed critics praised *Rocky* warmly. It came as a tasty achievement, said the *New Musical Express*, 'especially in an age when the only way it appears possible to launch a successful rock musical is to haul in Jesus Christ or some heavy wimp theme . . . It's sharp, short and sleazy, with a strong affection for Science Fiction/Horror "B" Movie Nostalgia and rock'n'roll.' The *Guardian* remarked 'this show won me over entirely because it achieves the rare feat of being witty and erotic at the same time.' The *Daily Mail* called it 'a superbly acid bon-bon'. *The Times*, more classically, described it as 'a dramatic aphrodisiac'.

Such an unqualified triumph rather surprised the promoters of a show which was originally intended as an experiment to keep some deserving actors in work and to finish its run by the end of July when a new production had to follow it at The Theatre Upstairs. Word spread very quickly and the remaining weeks were sold out. A small black market in tickets even began to flourish. The last night at The Theatre Upstairs was distinguished by the presence of Mick and Bianca Jagger in the audience and by the fact that the show could not go on in the absence of an understudy for Rayner Bourton as Rocky: some of the gold dust he sprinkled liberally over his body had trickled down beneath his lamé briefs and temporarily disabled him.

◀ RAYNER BOURTON

A new home was found for *The Rocky Horror Show*. On 14 August 1973, it opened not far away at the Classic Cinema in King's Road. With 270 seats on offer the old place could take four times the capacity of The Theatre Upstairs. There was no need of cosmetic alterations to reproduce the seedy atmosphere the production demanded: the Classic was already scheduled for demolition and exuded an aura of shabbiness that suited ideally.

It soon crumbled under pick and chain and hammer, but by that time *Rocky* had leapfrogged elsewhere and come to rest at another ancient Chelsea cinema,. this time the Essoldo. A lot of the money taken, and there had been a lot, was spent on the setting. Of the 400 seats available, 50 were torn out to make a central gangway for Frank's sensational entry. The show started there on 3 November.

The Rocky Horror Show had now established itself and attracted an enthusiastic following. People started coming back. Some saw it twenty times or so while it was still running in the King's Road, and one keen admirer, a woman, was reputed to have seen fifty performances. Wherever *Rocky* went in the first year of its existence, the elaborate system of platforms and gantry over the auditorium accompanied it. Flocks of masked hunchbacks wearing dark glasses went on escorting people to their seats and jabbing flimsy one-page programmes into their hands. Performances became an excuse for meeting friends made earlier in the run. Here came the chic and the fashionable. The news spread abroad and enticed Frenchmen, Italians and Americans to join the audience. A thoughtful entrepreneur organized *Rocky Horror Show* package tours from Paris.

When the London *Evening Standard*, as it was then known, made its drama awards for the year, *Rocky* was chosen as Best Musical of 1973.

The show moved once more, in 1979, to the Comedy Theatre in Panton Street off the Haymarket. At last it had found an auditorium that did it justice: with a seating capacity of 820 the theatre was big enough to meet the demand for seats yet small enough to preserve the intimacy and direct contact with the audience that were needed to sustain the original flavour. Here it played until 13 September 1980 and finally closed after a total run of 2,960 performances, although that was by no means the end of the affair.

A MEMBER OF THE AUDIENCE SUITABLY DRESSED

Frank has built and lost his creature – or has he?

Among the audience in the King's Road one evening was Britt Ekland. She saw *Rocky* a number of times and was so enraptured with it that she brought her then boyfriend, the American producer Lou Adler, to one of the shows. He liked it as much as she did. Within days he arranged to take over the American distribution rights.

Adler was the producer of the classic *Monterey Pop* and another cult film called *Brewster McCloud*. Having begun life as insurance man to Herb Alpert of Tijuana Brass, he then went into partnership with Herb. He had his own record label, Ode Records, himself wrote songs, and was part-owner of the Roxy night-club on Sunset Strip in Los Angeles. He never sent letters to people. He lived on the telephone.

The Rocky Horror Show made its American debut at the Roxy on 24 March 1974. Tim Curry and Richard O'Brien came over from the original London cast in their roles as Dr Frank'n'Furter and Riff-Raff. It ran there to packed houses for nine months. Film companies became interested. A deal was made for what was even then a very low budget of $1 million.

Filming began on the old Hammer lot at Bray in Berkshire. It was a cold November day in 1974, and the set, a dilapidated Victorian mansion which in the past had been the background of some forty creaking horror films, stood dark and cheerless under the blazing lights. There was no heating and draughts sighed interminably through dusty rooms. During the war the place had been a weekend home for General de Gaulle. Every now and then someone would open the drawer of a desk and find long-abandoned documents and letters.

The film was shot in six weeks. To help launch it with a bigger splash, the small-scale Roxy production was taken to Broadway and opened at the Belasco Theatre on 10 March 1975. The Belasco is a large and cavernous theatre topped by a yawning dome. *Rocky* was lost in it. The attempted mix of big spectacle and intimate cabaret did not succeed. Overstaged, muffled by the clink and chatter of waiters serving drinks, *Rocky* closed after fifty performances and lost $400,000.

The company which had sponsored the film of *Rocky* looked once more at the exotica with which it had saddled itself and thought again. But that is another story . . .

RICHARD O'BRIEN (RIFF-RAFF) AND TIM CURRY (FRANK) ▶

what ever happened to Fay Wray?

It is good to know that the creator of *The Rocky Horror Show* was born in Cheltenham, that most Georgian, most traditional, most English of towns. Richard O'Brien, or 'Ritz', first saw the light of day there on 25 March 1942, which makes him an Aries. When he was ten his family moved to New Zealand.

Richard was to stay there until the age of twenty-two. When he grew up his family envisaged a career in dairy farming for him. He, until the dreaded moment came, immersed himself in late-night double feature programmes at the local cinema. These gave him a lifelong passion for bad science-fiction films and B-movies. Soon they were complemented by an addiction to Dr Strange comics.

No one born after 1950 can truly appreciate the nostalgia that clings to the animated trademarks which used to introduce films of the period. Later generations, it is true, have become familiar with these old films on the small screen ever since Hollywood realized there was money to be made from selling their libraries to television. But fully to relish the MGM lion, the RKO radio transmitter and the scintillating globe of Universal you need first to have seen them, night after night, in picture houses where the beam of the projector sliced through floating wedges of thick tobacco smoke in an atmosphere rank with the smell of orange-peel and ice cream.

Metro-Goldwyn-Mayer films were introduced by a blasé lion which roared in muted tones and then, as if exhausted by the effort, turned its head to one side. Underneath it ran the legend *ARS GRATIA ARTIS*, 'art for art's sake', a slogan which today would be actionable under the Trades Description Laws. The lion was followed by Greta Garbo, or the Marx Brothers, or Spencer Tracey, or Clark Gable, or Joan Crawford, or Laurel and Hardy, for in its time MGM was the most successful of studios and claimed to employ 'all the stars in the heavens'.

Universal Studios sported a transparent globe surrounded by revolving glassy letters that spelt out the name against a background of what looked like prismatic ice clusters. This company could boast Deanna Durbin and a string of horror pictures centred on the villainous talents of Boris Karloff and Lon Chaney Jr. RKO Radio Pictures started with a transmitter bleeping out the firm's initials. Their product included Cary Grant and Katherine Hepburn. Warner Brothers intro-

◄ RICHARD O'BRIEN – PRETENDING TO BE BUTCH

RICHARD O'BRIEN –
THE MAN WHO PUT
FISHNETS
INTO HALLOWE'EN

KING KONG

duced themselves with an austere cartouche bearing the initials W.B. in 1930s'-style lettering. 'Working for Warners is like fucking a porcupine,' observed one disgruntled script writer. 'It's a hundred pricks against one.'

All these signs and symbols became a part of Richard O'Brien's youth and were absorbed into his culture, as they were with millions of other people growing up at that time. Later he was to incorporate what they stood for into *The Rocky Horror Show*, and more particularly into the opening number, 'Science Fiction'. The first line pays tribute to Michael Rennie, slim and handsome, whom he'd seen in *The Day the Earth Stood Still*, a sci-fi adventure where the pilot of a flying saucer arrives in Washington and frightens everyone to death with predictions of doom. At Saturday matinees O'Brien watched, episode by agonizing episode, the interminable exploits of Flash Gordon in the chunky per-

son of Buster Crabbe for ever battling against the cunning Emperor Ming on the planet Mars. 'And Flash Gordon was there, In silver underwear' refers to the quaint combination of woolly tights and close-fitting jumper worn by the hero.

Universal's glittering globe took Richard into the world of *The Invisible Man* played by the smooth British star Claude Rains, who, unseen throughout most of the film, was to gain a paradoxical immortality by appearing in person for only a few fleeting seconds. RKO thrilled the young film fan with *King Kong*, greatest of all the monster films. Brilliant tricks of photography, never equalled by re-makes and sequels, showed the giant gorilla nursing Fay Wray in his vast paws and then, on top of the Empire State Building, defying squadrons of aircraft sent to shoot him down. And whatever, as Dr Frank enquires, happened to Fay Wray? After starring in many 1930s' movies she made a few television programmes and her last film, *Hell on Frisco Bay*, in 1955. Today she lives retired in her Los Angeles home and spends much of her time answering fan letters from the generations as they grow up and succumb to the cult of King Kong.

Oh, at the late-night double feature picture show!

'Anne Francis stars in *Forbidden Planet*,' sings Magenta. This refers to a science-fiction epic dished up by MGM and remotely based on *The Tempest*. 'It's a pity,' remarked *The New Yorker*, 'they didn't lift some of Shakespeare's language.'

Leo G. Carrol ('I knew Leo G. Carrol was over a barrel') starred in *Tarantula*, an extravaganza about an infected spider which takes on giant proportions. Another creepy that stayed in Richard's memory was *The Day of The Triffids* featuring Janette Scott as the heroine and a platoon of horrid living plants which take over a world devastated by meteorites. Even more spectacular was *When Worlds Collide*, in which a space-ship is piloted by creatures that can transmute into human beings. *It Came From Outer Space*, with breathtaking special effects by George Pal ('Said George Pal to his bride, I'm going to give you some terrible thrills'), showed a rogue planet smashing up the universe. Twenty-five years later Richard could still remember vividly *Night of the Demon* and its hero Dana Andrews whose wooden good looks decorated many pictures of the time. Here a necromancer summoned up a giant devil from the Middle Ages to overcome his enemies. Among his occult practices was that of casting the runes, a feature celebrated in the lines:

> *Dana Andrews said prunes*
> *Gave him the runes*
> *And passing them used lots of*
> *skills . . .*

It was, however, *Frankenstein* that made the deepest impression on Richard as he sat transfixed at late-night picture shows. The film, produced in 1931 at Universal, is taken from a novel written early last century by Mary Shelley, nineteen-year-old wife of the poet. She intended it as a Promethean allegory on the nature of artistic creation and the moral consequences of scientific discovery. Frankenstein, creator of the monster, is accursed through having made something which brings him only ruin and sorrow. In a nuclear age the lesson of *Frankenstein* is starkly contemporary, although Hollywood, naturally, was more interested in the baroque trappings of this classic tale than in its philosophical implications.

The first, and probably the best, of all monsters was a British actor who understandably adopted the pseudonym Boris Karloff in preference to his unfortunate baptismal name of William Pratt. In private life a gentle, home-loving cricket player, on the screen, wearing make-up that took four hours each day to apply, he was able to suggest all sorts of lurking horrors. Since then there have been over ninety different film versions of the novel. In some of them Frankenstein has been given a bride, in others a son. Over the years he has met the Wolf Man and the once popular comedians Abbott and Costello. In *The Rocky Horror Show* he reaches his apotheosis as Dr Frank'n'Furter.

Always bracketed with *Frankenstein* is *Dracula*, which comes from the excruciatingly bad novel by Bram Stoker, once upon a time manager to Sir Henry Irving. *Dracula* is, indeed, so bad as to achieve a certain perfection even though it might not qualify for George Orwell's distinction of 'good bad literature'. Yet, unlike many better novels, it has established itself in folklore because of the gripping yarn it tells. The blood-sucking vampire is the central figure of close to 150 films and is beaten, as a character, only by Sherlock Holmes, the subject of more than 180. Again it was Universal Studios who launched the most famous version with Bela Lugosi, the Hungarian actor, in the role of the long-toothed Transylvanian Count. Many sequels, as in the case of *Frankenstein*, gave Dracula a son and various brides. Inevitably he made the acquaintance of Abbott and Costello. Dracula is thoroughly bisexual, for he has graced both the hetero *Naked World of Harrison Marks* and the gay *Does Dracula Really Suck*? All this has been useful grooming for his contribution to *The Rocky Horror Show* and to Frank's 'I'm just a sweet transvestite from transexual Transylvania.' And if Janet addresses Rocky as 'creature of the night', she does but echo Dracula's remark when the cry of the wolves is heard at dawn in the Transylvanian valleys: 'Listen to them — the children of the night. What music they make.'

RICHARD O'BRIEN (RIFF-RAFF), RAYNER BOURTON (ROCKY), TIM CURRY (FRANK)

in just seven days

Besides the horror and sci-fi movies Richard absorbed in the comforting darkness of New Zealand flea-pits there were the technicoloured spectaculars which, throughout the 1950s, came in their dozens from Italian studios. They chronicled the labours of Hercules, the adventures of Goliath, the last days of Pompeii and anything, in short, that gave an excuse for magic carpets or an earthquake or three. Their hero was Steve Reeves, first 'Mr World', then 'Mr Universe', and at all times a handsome piece of meat with rippling muscles and inordinate thighs. 'If you want something visual that's not too abysmal,' suggests Frank, 'We could take in an old Steve Reeves movie.'

Steve Reeves as the inspiration for Rocky, Frank's creation, is linked with an advertisement O'Brien saw repeatedly in his favourite comics. It showed the magnificent torso and bulging biceps of strong man Charles Atlas. To readers of his advertisment the confident Mr Charles Atlas promised that, if they followed his muscle building plan, he could make a man of them in just seven days. His message was further dramatized in a cartoon strip that showed a weakling at the seaside being insulted by a well set-up athlete who contemptuously kicked sand in his face. After training himself on the Atlas plan the former drip acquired muscle, stood up to the bully and won over the girls who crowded round him to admire his noble physique. The advertisement, as much a classic as 'They laughed when I sat down at the piano' (though laughter turned to admiration when the hero played as beautifully as Paderewski thanks to the advertiser's mail-order lessons), ran for decades unchanged and is the reason Mr Atlas died rich. Frank pays tribute to him in the Charles Atlas song:

> A weakling weighing ninety-eight
>   pounds
> Got sand in his face when kicked to the
>   ground
> His girl split on him
> So soon in the gym
> The sweat from his pores
> As he worked for his cause
> Made him glisten and gleam
> And with massage and steam
> He was thin but quite clean
> He was in good shape.
> But the wrong shape.
> He ate nutritious high-protein
> And swallowed raw eggs
> Tried to build up his shoulders
> His chest, arms and legs
> Then a magazine advert with a new
>   muscle plan
> Said in just seven days I can make you
>   a man . . .
> But a deltoid and a bicep
> A hot groin and a tricep
> Makes me shake
> Makes me wanna take
> Charles Atlas by the hand.
> In just seven days I can make you a
>   man.

And who is the Lilly St Cyr whose name is invoked during that poignant exchange between Brad and Janet?

> It's beyond me
> Help me Mommy.
> God bless Lilly St Cyr.'

Whether or not she took her name from the French military training establishment, the famous equivalent of Sandhurst, the facts are that she was a renowned American strip-tease artist in the 1940s — blonde, svelte, cute. Later, drawing on the practical knowledge acquired in the exercise of her art over the years, she founded a women's underwear shop in Hollywood and promoted it with the message: 'Fabulous Fashion Sensations from the Undie-World of Lilli St Cyr.' After a period of time she subsided into prosperous retirement at her Los Angeles home.

STEVE REEVES IN ONE OF HIS EPIC ROLES

CHARLES ATLAS ▶

I can make you a man

Yes! I Turn Weaklings into HE-MEN!

Charles Atlas

Holder of the title, "The World's Most Perfectly Developed Man."

Let Me Make YOU a NEW MAN in Just 15 Minutes a Day

YES, Sir, *that's my job!* I "RE-BUILD" skinny, run-down weaklings—fellows so embarrassed by their second-rate physical condition that they always hang back, let others walk off with the best jobs, the prettiest girls, the most fun and popularity. I turn weaklings like these into HE-MEN—REAL SPECIMENS OF HANDSOME, MUSCULAR MANHOOD—overflowing with pep, power, vitality! I'll PROVE that, in only 15 minutes a day, I can make YOU a NEW MAN too!

I'll Prove What I Say

I know what it's like to have a body others laugh at. I myself was once a 7-stone weakling—timid, ill-at-ease, ashamed to strip for sports or a swim. Then I discovered "Dynamic-Tension." It changed me from a 7-stone weakling into the winner of the title, "THE WORLD'S MOST PERFECTLY DEVELOPED MAN." Since then my "Dynamic - Tension" has transformed thousands of other weak, no-muscle men into real Atlas Champions

What I'll Do For YOU!

Where do YOU want solid, tough LIVE MUSCLE? Are you fat and flabby? Or skinny and gawky? Are you short-winded, sluggish, always tired? I'll give you a sledge-hammer fist and mighty forearm. Add inches to your biceps. Put a coat of muscle straight across your stomach. Change those legs that are "always tired" into mighty, vigorous columns of speed and stamina. You'll begin to know what it feels like to really LIVE!

SEND FOR FREE BOOK

Post coupon right now. I'll send you a FREE COPY of my famous illustrated book, "Everlasting Health and Strength." In it I talk to you in straight-from-the-shoulder language—show you actual photographs of myself and other fellows who became NEW MEN, my way. You'll read the story of "Dynamic-Tension"— what it has done for others, what I'm ready to PROVE, in only 15 minutes a day, it can do for YOU! Send for this book today

CHARLES ATLAS, Dept. 147-E,
2, Dean Street. London. W.1.

I want the proof that your system of "Dynamic-Tension" will help make a New Man of me—give me a healthy, husky body and big muscular development. Send me your free book, "Everlasting Health and Strength" AT ONCE!

Name *(Please print or write plainly)*

Address

it was great...

Richard's education was complete – or at least the more important part of it. Memories of his early life in Cheltenham were in time overlaid by impressions of New Zealand where he grew up. He liked it there, the idyllic scenery, the relaxed existence, the native music of the Maoris and their resonant chants and stylized dances. Horses interested him and he took up riding at which he quickly became proficient. Cows he found much less fascinating, especially when his parents, with the best of intentions, enrolled him on a three-year course to learn dairy farming.

At a quite early age he preferred acting to breeding cows. Somewhere he discovered the unique pleasure to be got from making people laugh and from winning over an audience. As the veteran comic actor Edward Everett Horton once remarked: 'The older I grow in this wonderful profession of which I have the honour to be a member, the more convinced I become that you can listen to waves on the shore of a brook in the forest, the wind in the trees, or the rain on the roof, but there is no more thrilling, no more exhilarating sound in all of nature than applause, and I never get enough of it.'

...when it all began

That was how the future author of *The Rocky Horror Show* felt. For a time he studied The Method, a technique evolved by the American director Lee Strasberg from Stanislavsky's teaching that the actor must forget everything about himself except the role he is playing. Then Richard developed his own individual line of comedy, having first taken Peter Sellers as one of his models. His aim, pure and simple, was to entertain people and inspire laughter. It is an ambition that has been shared at one time or another by Aristophanes, Shakespeare, Molière and Bernard Shaw.

Once he had qualified, on paper, as a dairy farmer, he felt he had done his duty and he left New Zealand where his parents, two brothers, sisters and many nieces and nephews still live. In the 1960s, at the age of twenty-two, he came back to his native country and settled in London. He earned his living to begin with as a barber and as a dustman. His earliest film appearance was in *Carry on Cowboy*, for which his skill in handling and riding horses qualified him as a stunt man. At evening classes he persisted with his study of acting and, during the day, played a small part in the film *Casino Royale*.

Next came a role in the touring company of the American tribal-rock musical *Hair* and then a part in Sean Kenny's production of *Gulliver's Travels*. After which, he says, 'I was supposed to take over the role of Herod in *Jesus Christ Superstar*, but I had terrible doubts from the start. The previous actor was much more showbiz and very out-going, whereas I try to work with undercurrents. What happened was that I went on for one night and was terrible. I told the director of *Superstar*, Jim Sharman, that I'd written this musical — all science fiction and rock tunes — and he said he'd like to stage it. I had nothing else to do, so we went ahead.'

During his time as an out-of-work actor in London Richard had been able to renew acquaintance at late-night television screenings with the films he remembered from his New Zealand youth. These, together with the Marvel Comics he used to read in the flowerpower era — 'Dr Strange was the only one I really liked. But he's gone now,' he adds wistfully — had given him the inspiration for a rock opera. He found the music of shows in the mould of *Jesus Christ Superstar* too bland, too genteel. Rock, he felt, should ·be something more basic and sensual, like

the Marlboro cigarettes he smokes because he relishes the tang that percolates through his chest to sting deep down. Basing himself on three-chord guitar formations, he started to note down ideas for songs and passages of dialogue. The guitar is his favourite instrument and he plays it still.

Jim Sharman left *Jesus Christ Superstar* to direct *The Unseen Hand*, a new play by Sam Shepard at The Theatre Upstairs. Richard was engaged to play the part of Willie The Space Freak and discovered that Shepard had drawn on familiar sources: old B-movies, comics, science fiction and horror films. He talked further with Sharman about his own ideas for a rock musical.

The son of a showman who ran a big circus in Australia, Jim Sharman had already made a name for himself in experimental theatre both there and in England. He directed the Australian productions of *Hair* and *Jesus Christ Superstar*. Among his more avant-garde ventures were a revue associated with *OZ* magazine and a spectacle that alternated disco dancing with performances of Jean Genet's *The Maids* over a period of six hours without intermission. The Genet project lost money but helped fulfil one of Sharman's ambitions, which was to bring the theatre closer in line with other types of live entertainment.

Sharman had already made a 16mm colour film with the title *Shirley Thompson Versus the Aliens*. It was a pioneer exploration of science fiction in terms of rock and roll, and that, maybe, is one reason why Richard's ideas caught his interest. At first the play was called *They Came from Denton High*. This changed to *The Rocky Hooroar Show* and eventually settled as *The Rocky Horror Show*.

A tape of Richard singing 'Science Fiction Double Feature' with his own guitar accompaniment found its way to Michael White, the independent theatre producer. He was immediately intrigued and wanted to hear more. A vague outline of the plot about Dr Frank'n'Furter and the innocents in the decaying mansion, together with reference to the old movies and Hollywood cult figures he'd always loved, convinced him that this was something he very much wanted to do. He spent £2000 on the production and booked it into The Theatre Upstairs. 'I had no idea,' he says, 'that Sharman would come up with one of the most brilliant musical productions of all time.'

it's so dreamy—oh fantasy free me!

The Rocky Horror Show began its long life on that darkling night in 1973, a date which has passed into theatrical history. '*Rocky* is a piece of trivia that's appealed to a lot of people and given them a lot of pleasure,' says Richard modestly. 'I guess you could say I'm proud to have done that. The nicest thing about it, though, is that now I can call up anybody anywhere, tell them who I am and get five minutes of their time.'

When people mention the sexual ambiguity of the play he remarks:

> *It's foolish to define people by whom they sleep with, and it would be irresponsible to see it as a testament to sexual promiscuity. It's a moral tale, and 'Don't dream it, be it' means that if you want to sing, do it. If you want to write, drag that half-written novel out of the drawer and finish it. All our lives, people tell us we can't do it. We have to shut our ears and go ahead, and if what we do turns out to be a success, that's just icing on the cake. In the long run, no one can stop you but yourself.*

Since *Rocky* he has not rested on his laurels. His play *Disaster*, which brought together in the cast familiar faces from the original *Rocky* — Jonathan Adams (Narrator), Patricia Quinn (Magenta), Christopher Malcolm (Brad Majors) and himself — was set on a tropical island in the Bermuda Triangle. It involved an ambitious TV personality, her daughter, her ex-lover, a right-wing senator and a gay photographer who are all marooned on the island when their boat sinks and strands them. They then discover that two giant icebergs are converging slowly upon the island and, to complete the situation, that several tons of nuclear waste are floating in storage nearby. The impetus for the idea came from a friend who remarked: 'We've had all those disaster films. What's needed now is a disaster musical.'

His film *Shock Treatment* came out in 1979. It is an acrid satire on television set in the small American town of Denton (familiar name) where the whole community has turned into a non-stop TV show in which everyone takes part. Barry Humphries, alias Dame Edna Everage, played the role of a crazy Viennese psychiatrist and Richard himself, as a lunatic doctor in charge of an asylum, delivered one of the best one-liners ever written: 'Trust me. I'm a doctor.'

Other work has included a television play, *A Hymn From Jim*, a short story for children called *Uggers and Mee*, and the rock musical *T. Zee* at the Royal Court. Meanwhile he has continued to act. In Sam Shepard's *Mickey Mouse Now* he played the title role as a fifty-year-old alcoholic opposite Little Nell as Minnie Mouse. They also appeared together in Derek Jarman's punk movie *Jubilee*. His latest starring part was in the very successful cabaret-type musical *The News* at the Paramount City Theatre in London. 'He is a figure from some Gothic nightmare,' said a critic, 'and it is his presence which holds the evening together.' Gothic, too, was his acting in the recent television serial *Robin of Sherwood*, where as Gulran the sorcerer his spectral shadow and eldritch sneer cast a chill over the forest.

He still enjoys the tacky science fiction films and B-movies that inspired *The Rocky Horror Show*, especially the ones featuring Broderick Crawford. Crawford was a large, beefy American actor who moved from playing small-time gangsters and cowboy desperadoes to corrupt tycoons and politicians. His shifty eyes and suspicious mouth appeared in over 100 films between 1937 and 1981, occasionally on the side of justice, more often defending some shady venture against nosey police detectives. Richard O'Brien thinks of this type of film with affection. 'The makers usually know what star they want for the picture but they can't afford them. So they get some third-rate guy to impersonate the star. So it works on at least two different levels. I like bad acting. There's a kind of innocence about those films.'

It is also the innocence which helps to give *The Rocky Horror Show* some of its appeal. Says Brad to Janet, wide-eyed, serious: 'Didn't we pass a castle back down the road a few miles?' When Frank reveals the existence of the sonic transducer, an 'audio vibratory physiomolecular transport device', Dr Scott voices the sort of line that has become a classic in science fiction movies: 'It seems our friend here has found a way of perfecting it — a device that is capable of breaking down solid matter and then projecting it through space and who knows, perhaps even time itself.' The finishing touch is his desperate cry: 'We've got to get out of this trap before this decadence saps our wills. I've got to be strong and try to hang on or my mind may well snap . . .' Many a time and oft, dearly beloved kitsch, have the 'goodies' spoken like that at climactic moments.

SHOCK TREATMENT POSTER ▶

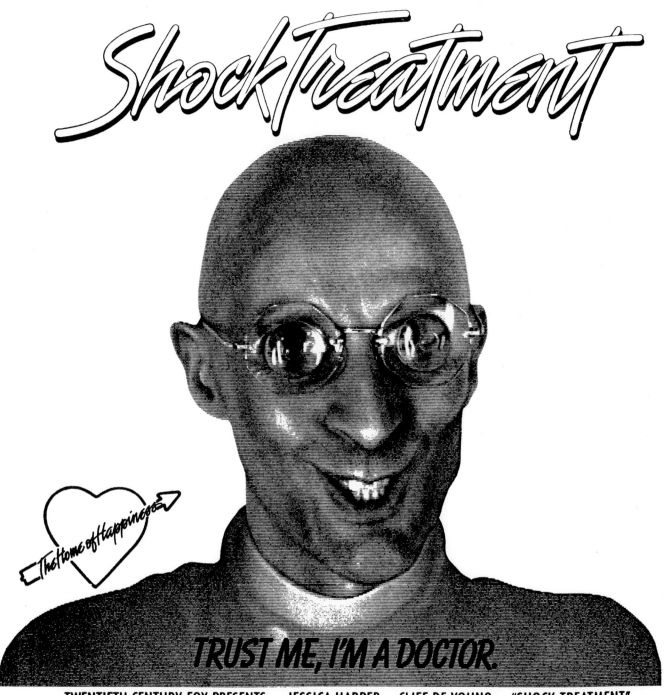

25

Rose tints my world

It is an endearing tradition of the theatre that comedians, in private life, should be miserable creatures and that actors who specialize in playing villains should, offstage, be the nicest and gentlest of people. Richard O'Brien is no exception. The stage and film persona of the sinister Riff-Raff, the eerie psychopath, vanishes to be replaced by a civilized and generous companion. The voice is soft and low, the features small and delicately shaped. The manner is courteous, almost shy. In the world of showbiz, where malice flourishes, he is benevolent and sincere. From time to time a flash of zany humour peeps out.

Today he lives with his family in a converted Victorian terrace house near Lavender Hill in Battersea. From the street the only visible indication of who might be within is the psychedelic lettering of the street number on the fanlight. Once over the threshold you are in a dream home cunningly adapted for space, elegance, light. A shade of blue predominates and an aura of rococo decadence fills the place. On the wall hang Sunday school pictures and examples of Gothic religious art. He also collects sheet music covers from the 1920s and 1930s, uniformly framed and thematically linked by the word 'blue' which recurs in all the song titles.

Religious art gives him a feeling of great calm. 'I suppose I am a religious person,' says the author of Dr Frank and Riff-Raff. 'I think that man created God rather than God created man. Maybe He exists because we believe He does. It's the ultimate mystery, better than Agatha Christie.'

He lives with his second wife Jane, a beautiful and talented costume designer, by whom he has a son. How long have they been married? About four years, he thinks. There is also another son, Linus, born in 1972 of his first marriage to Kimi Wong whom he met while touring *Hair*. She later appeared as one of the Transylvanians in the film of *The Rocky Horror Show*. Together, as 'Kimi and Ritz', they made several records. But of this marriage, which ended in the mid-1970s, he says; 'My lips are sealed.'

When he isn't acting he likes to draw and paint his obsessions — rude angels. Musically he is still faithful to the guitar and plays rock'n'roll always. Buddy Holly is one of his favourite artists, but most of all he admires Otis Redding.

At weekends and during holidays he makes off with his family to the house he owns in Dorset — when, that is, a summons to Los Angeles on a script-writing expedition doesn't intervene, or when daily performances in the theatre (twice nightly on Friday and Saturday) don't cramp his style. The huge success of *The Rocky Horror Show* has failed to change an unusually sweet and simple nature. 'It's amazing that some of the kids mouthing the words of "Science Fiction" from the show were only about six when it came out,' he observes in wonderment.

RICHARD O'BRIEN AS FAMILY MAN

from lighthouse to loot

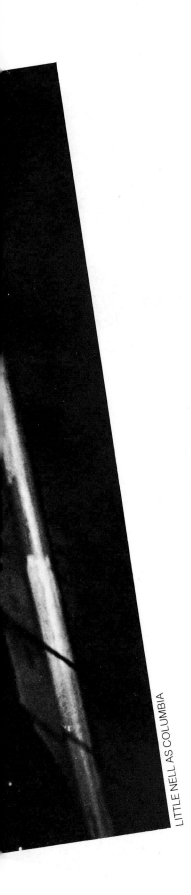

LITTLE NELL AS COLUMBIA

When a manufacturer launches a new soap or a new washing powder he knows that there are lots of people about who buy washing powder and soap. His only problem is to identify, with the aid of market research, where they can be found. An impresario, on the other hand, is guided by intuition alone. He comes across an idea, likes it, backs it with his own or other people's money and fervently hopes that the public will agree with him. He knows that the surest way of losing money, apart from throwing it into the Thames, is to bet on race-horses or invest in show business.

The London impresario and producer Michael White has been leading this dangerous existence for the past twenty-five years. He is cool, laconic, but gives the impression of living on the edge of a volcano. *The Rocky Horror Show* has been one of his biggest successes. 'It is the only show I have ever done that I can watch time and time again – I must have seen it a hundred times,' he says. 'If the audience is particularly interesting it takes on a whole new flavour. And it is snappy; only an hour and twenty minutes, non-stop, no interval. Every three minutes you are being socked with another song or event. Everything about it works. *The Rocky Horror Show* is critic-proof.'

Born in 1936, White had a cosmopolitan childhood and youth. His first job was on the New York Stock Exchange where he worked as a messenger boy. New York after hours in that pre-drugs era was mostly innocent but no less fascinating and haunted by the shadowy presence of people like James Dean and Jackson Pollock. He left the Stock Exchange to write a novel in the solitude of a lighthouse near Connecticut. This novel, together with four others, has not yet been published.

The lighthouse owner's sister ran a theatre in Westport and suggested he work there for the summer. Having begun a lifelong affair with the theatre at the Comédie Française and acquired a wide knowledge of the repertoire the hard way on the cheapest wooden seats, White eagerly accepted the offer. An early lesson he learned was that in any theatrical production there is as much drama off-stage as on.

A year or so later he came back to England and worked as assistant to Sir Peter Daubeny who had, by then, made his World Theatre Seasons the most sumptuous events of their kind.

The young man he described as 'my ardent and ambitious assistant' left him after a five-year apprenticeship to launch his own first venture, an American play called *The Connection*. Its subject was drug addiction, something which in early 1960s' Britain was little known. The naturalistic style was brutally powerful and highly disturbing. So shocked was public reaction that White and some of the cast who had gone to dine at a well-known restaurant were asked to leave. The play survived no more than forty-six performances.

Over the years White followed the same dogged policy of backing the plays he believed in. An obscure Russian play he liked was adapted as *Son of Oblomov* and featured Spike Milligan who, wearing a nightgown, happened by mistake to kick off one of his slippers and send it flying into the stalls. 'Unless you've got three feet,' shouted Spike, 'can you throw me back my slipper?' The first-night audience was completely won over.

By the mid-1960s White had taken on an American import known as 'happenings', random events which involved naked girls rolling in paint and spraying detergent over the audience. Others were pummelled with wet fish and wrapped up in bags. After presenting a hilarious season of Yoko Ono he managed, just, to avoid being caught up in the notorious film called *Bottoms* which she made with John Lennon.

Joe Orton's *Loot* followed, a masterpiece of black comedy with action provided by a plot based on the need to hide a mother's corpse in a cupboard. The controversy this inspired was minor compared with the sensation caused by *Oh Calcutta!*, an erotic revue which the late Ken Tynan, journalist and drama critic, put together with the aid of writers such as Orton, Samuel Beckett and others. The topics included a homage to striptease, knickers, bottoms and a generous variety of private obsessions which, until then, had never been revealed on a public stage.

the dirtiest show in town

Some time afterwards Michael White presented *The Dirtiest Show in Town*, an American production with what must be one of the most brilliantly commercial titles ever. It had a scene intended to represent copulation. One evening, unknown to the audience, the actor concerned, perhaps bored with make-believe, did the real thing, much to the outraged annoyance of the actress. Only the most delicate negotiations avoided a scandal.

Another venture by Michael White Ltd proved the truth of the old saying about swings and roundabouts. *Jeeves* was based on the popular Wodehouse stories and had a script by Alan Ayckbourn with music by Andrew Lloyd Webber, two of the most bankable names in the English theatre. It flopped dismally.

Since then Michael White has presented *Sleuth, A Chorus Line* and *The Pirates of Penzance*, among many others. He has always been a film buff and his career in the cinema began with *Monty Python and the Holy Grail*. In the life of every impresario there are many cherished projects which, for various reasons, never come to fruition. One of them was a film he planned to make with the Sex Pistols. It was to have been called *Who Killed Bambi?*

With his reputation for daring and originality, Michael White was the ideal producer for *The Rocky Horror Show*. On the strength of the barest outline he sensed right away the possibilities of the initial idea. Preparations began with much of the dialogue being written as rehearsals went along. The musical arrangements for a group made up of three guitars, saxophones, drums, piano/organ and synthesizer were devised by Richard Hartley, composer of incidental music for Michael Caine's film *The Romantic Englishwoman*. Brian Thomson designed the scenery of Frank's castle and Sue Blane dressed the show. She later did the costumes for the National Theatre's production of *Guys and Dolls*, although for some time both she and Thomson found it difficult to convince people that they could do other things beside their striking *Rocky Horror Show* designs.

Michael White took no more than a passing interest in rehearsals. When the preview date arrived he looked in to find, with delight, that the show managed to combine so many of the features that had captivated him at the beginning: the feeling of liberation, the borderline sexuality, the urge, in short, to 'be it', not 'dream it'. His own children, he discovered, wanted to see it again and again, though none of them was more than ten years old at the time. The same thing was to happen with the generations that followed.

Rocky duly transferred from the Theatre Upstairs to the Classic Cinema. The money made, and a lot more, was spent on transferring to the Essoldo. The owners of the Essoldo offered it to White. He was not, however, attracted to owning property and did not feel at ease with those who dealt in it. He wishes, now, that he had accepted the offer. What he should have done, he says, was to move straight into a West End theatre. Loyalty to the show, which caused him to make expensive alterations to the cinema, made him stay put.

While Richard O'Brien and Tim Curry were away playing their original roles in the American production, Robert Longden and Ziggy Byfield took over as Riff-Raff and Frank. A biographical note in the programme revealed that Longden had begun his career as a stripper in a leper colony, after which he understudied the front half of a horse for the Royal Shakespeare Company where he also played the part of a duck. He was, added the programme, of a happy disposition. Ziggy's biography was terser. 'For details,' it read, 'enquire at stage door.'

Michael White went on to produce *Annie* and to live happily ever after.

TIM CURRY (FRANK) DEALING WITH EDDIE ▶

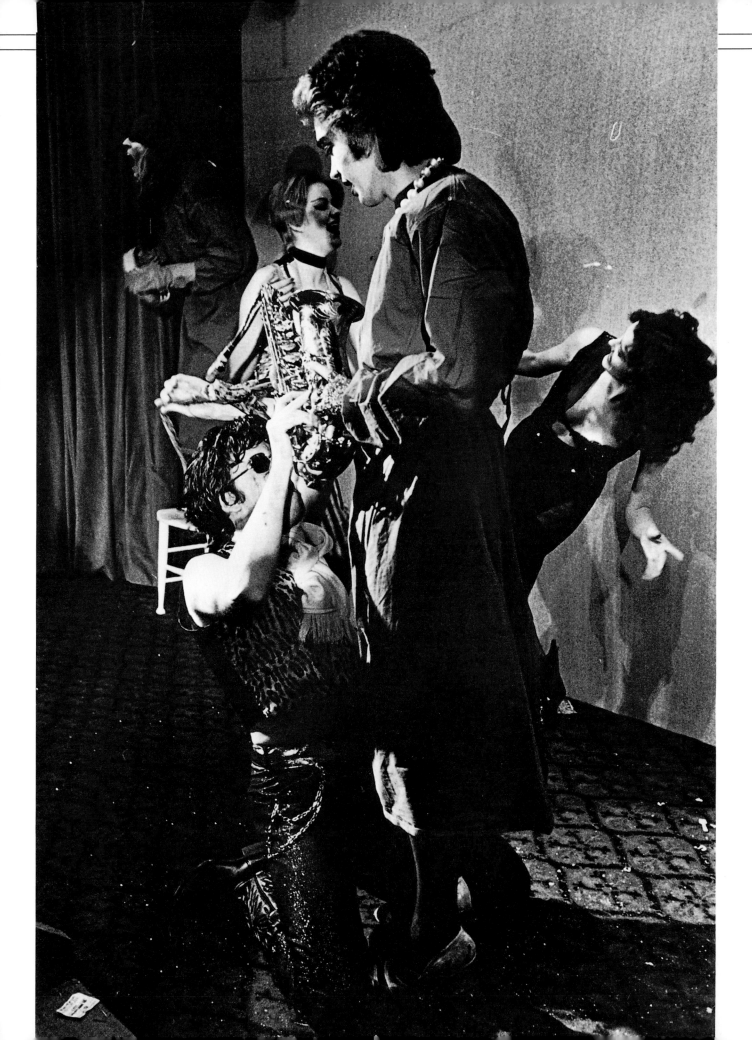

Rocky goes to Hollywood

Now that all the old showmen who built up Hollywood are dead the remaining film companies are not normally distinguished for their enterprise or their daring. If an independent producer wants to make a film about blue-nosed whales and asks for support, he is met with jeers and derision. If he goes ahead on his own and engineers a vast box-office success, within days all the other studios are making films about blue-nosed whales.

The initial staging of *The Rocky Horror Show* in America awoke interest from several film companies. Lou Adler handled the negotiations. He impressed Michael White with his relaxed charm and laid-back style of doing business. Although he never wore anything but jeans they were always expensive. A sweater was his permanent uniform, though knitted by hand and decorated with original designs by the artist. His boots came from a legendary craftsman in Texas. A large and anarchic black beard, together with the jeans, probably explain why an important film executive once arrived at a meeting and haughtily observed, staring right at him, that Adler was late.

The president of one big film company was invited to a performance of *The Rocky Horror Show* at which Adler had carefully planted enthusiastic fans among the audience. The tycoon did not really understand what was going on but agreed to spend $1 million on filming the show. He is no longer president.

The Hammer studios in Bray, Berkshire, were chosen as the venue for shooting. The film was to be presented, in England, as a White-Adler production, and in America as an Adler-White venture. Suddenly, less than a fortnight before filming was to begin, a palace revolution occurred at the film company. The new management, uneasy with the strange project their predecessors had taken on, demanded more information.

The venture had reached a crucial point. 'Film companies often try to make new conditions in a deal at the last moment,' explains Michael White, 'and, because a producer is at that stage committed and must have the money to start the film, he usually has to agree to whatever they want. But one of the great moments of my life had arrived. Lou and I were in a position to raise the entire million ourselves . . . ' After a brief Sunday morning encounter by a Hollywood swimming pool the managements, somewhat dazed, agreed to go ahead. A few weeks later the head of production, who happened to be a son of the late film star Alan Ladd, came to Bray and looked around the set. He left in a state of acute bewilderment.

The film was completed in six weeks. At such a pace there were bound to be moments of weariness and irritability. It was difficult to work up an energetic rock'n'roll number at 9.00 a.m. on a glacial December morning. There were, however, moments of charm, as on that October day, which would have been the eighty-first birthday of Charles Atlas, when the cast gathered round and sang the Charles Atlas song – 'In just seven days I can make you a man' – as a tribute to the ancient superhero.

◀ RAYNER BOURTON AS THE NEWLY-BORN ROCKY

lewd and lascivious lips

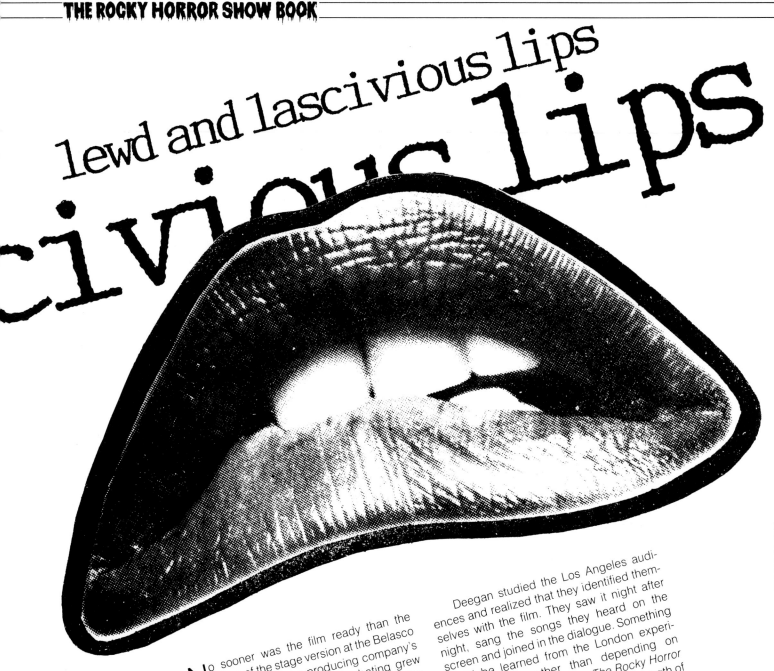

No sooner was the film ready than the failure of the stage version at the Belasco Theatre increased the producing company's alarm. The doubts already incubating grew into panic. Distributors and exhibitors alike did not know what to do with this ugly duckling. A trailer was made featuring the moving lips which open the film. The chairman of the board was horrified and ordered the instant removal of the 'lewd, lascivious' things.

One of the company's employees who attended previews arranged in the spring of 1975 was a twenty-six-year-old executive called Tim Deegan. Because he was young, and because no one else wanted the job, he had been given the unwelcome task of promoting the film. Only in Los Angeles did it do well. Everywhere else it was a failure. Exhibitors complained that audiences were as small as fifty. What they did not realize was that these fifty people came back again and again.

Deegan studied the Los Angeles audiences and realized that they identified themselves with the film. They saw it night after night, sang the songs they heard on the screen and joined in the dialogue. Something could be learned from the London experience, where, rather than depending on advertising and hyperbole, *The Rocky Horror Show* had turned into a cult on the strength of word-of-mouth recommendation.

There was no need, he saw, for the heavy promotion required to sell a new Stallone film or the latest Robert Redford epic. Neither was it necessary for exhibitors to dream up exotic campaigns with the aim of attracting audiences. The film was exotic enough on its own. A few discreet slogans were released and a handful of dollars set aside for expenses when the film opened at midnight showings in the Waverley Theatre, New York, on 1 April 1976. Box-office takings grew.

AUDIENCE LOOK-ALIKES

AUDIENCE LOOK-ALIKES

The figures persuaded other exhibitors to take a risk. They did so, one by one, and soon the film was enjoying long runs throughout the USA and Canada. Deegan and Lou Adler knew that time was needed for it to flower. By underselling, by allowing audiences to find out for themselves, they let *Rocky* make its own way. It would have been folly to send it out on general release. The magic formula was midnight showings, or what is known as 'the werewolf circuit'.

The audiences who went to these midnight showings began to evolve their own rituals. While Frank and Riff-Raff acted out their drama on the screen above, in the auditorium below sat spectators dressed in look-alike gear: half a dozen Franks, Riff-Raffs, Janets, Brads, Magentas, Columbias, Eddies, Dr Scotts and even stiff-necked Narrators. At crucial points in the narrative they helped the action along. During the wedding scene at the beginning they imitated the guests by throwing rice, and when Rocky and Frank set off for the bridal chamber they sped them on their way with showers of confetti. The dialogue, which they had come to know by heart through repeated viewings, was intercut with chants in unison. Thus, at Magenta's line 'Master, dinner is prepared', they would shout back: 'And we helped'. In some cinemas the management found they did not need to stock up with paper for the lavatories, since, at Brad's cry of 'Great Scott!' when Dr Scott enters the scene, rolls of toilet paper were thrown in abundance. In others people roared up and down the aisles on motor bikes to salute Eddie's arrival.

Although Tim Deegan could never quite understand the appeal of the show, he knew that midnight screenings were the key to its success. The film was too individual for casual viewing. It needed the atmosphere, the sense of 'belonging' that fans built up in a way that no other film has ever encouraged. If *Rocky* were to be generally released or made available on video cassettes the spell would be broken. Audience participation was the secret.

Not only as a cult film but also as a moneymaker *Rocky* continues to break records. In ten years it has grossed almost as much as *Gone With The Wind* and still shows no signs of flagging. The merchandising activity it has generated is brisk and enterprising. The obvious items include badges, calendars, posters, T-shirts and postcards. There has even been talk of Dr Frank'n'Furter in the shape of a Barbie doll.

are you a virgin?

All history is, in a way, hindsight, and on looking back over the years it is obvious that a fan club would have had to be founded. It began in September 1977, and was the work of a group who regularly attended showings at the Waverley Theatre in New York where the audience participation rites had become formalized with the passing of time. The president is Sal Piro, a native of New Jersey City who in early life was a teacher of Catholic theology. He has also been an actor, a professional writer of greetings cards and a tournament chess player, all of which constituted admirable preparation for his great role in life.

A genial man of limitless enthusiasm, he presides as MC at Friday and Saturday showings. By now he has seen the film well over 1000 times and his knowledge of the smallest detail in it is encyclopaedic. Under his sympathetic guidance the audience-participation dialogue and activity have been firmly established and ritualized. Everyone knows that when the Narrator appears the correct line to shout is: 'Where's your fuckin' neck?' Everyone knows, too, that the proper greeting to Brad is: 'Asshole!' and that when Frank laments 'It's not easy having a good time,' the remark to make is: 'Try Disney-world.'

Those who see the film for the first time are classified as 'virgins'. A helpful list of props is supplied for their use. Among the items specified are rice to be thrown at the wedding, newspapers to be held over the head when Janet does likewise in 'There's a light over at the Frankenstein place,' water pistols to imitate the rain, candles to be lit, rubber gloves to be snapped in sympathy with Frank during the emergence of Rocky, rattles to accompany the Transylvanian conventioneers, confetti, rolls of Scott tissue, toast to be thrown when Frank proposes the toast, a party hat to be donned at the dinner, a bell, and cards for brandishing at Frank's line 'cards for sorrow, cards for pain'. A final note warns against the habit of throwing prunes and hot dogs. This, it warns, is not a good idea since it encourages mice and damages the screen.

Fans are reminded that a proper etiquette should always be observed. The fun of throwing things should not result in damaging other people, their make-up, costumes or cinema furnishings. Members of the audience who dress up are not to be mocked unkindly. You should not be jealous or annoyed if someone else is attired as the character you have chosen for yourself — after all, the show doesn't belong to you. If outsiders come to the performance you must refrain from shouting them down if they speak different lines; indeed, they might be better than your own. And the rude salutations to the Narrator and Brad, though amusing when first heard, tend to bore if overdone.

Sal leads the performance as if he were a priest conducting a service. The hallowed lines are mouthed with force but with discipline. 'I want to come again,' moans Frank. 'So does Brad!' the audience roars in sonorous tones. 'In just seven days,' proclaims Frank. 'That's a week,' they add helpfully. 'Come inside,' the sinister Riff-Raff invites. 'I don't care where you come, as long as you clean it up,' they shout. 'Cross my heart and hope to die,' swears Frank. 'Stick a dildoe in my eye,' they chorus. 'Brad,' enquires Dr Scott, 'what are you doing here?' 'Oh, just fucking around,' they reply.

As national spokesman for the club, Sal edits and contributes to *The Transylvanian*, the official fan magazine. It features news about the cast, details of publications, shops where merchandise can be bought, articles, puzzles and crosswords. Fans are invited to distribute newsletters and to act as official representatives in the hundreds of cinemas up and down the country where midnight screenings take place. Every item issued is stamped with the formal 'Richard O'Brien Seal of Approval'.

FAN CLUB MEMBERSHIP CARD

THE ROCKY HORROR PICTURE SHOW

OFFICIAL FAN CLUB

1982 OFFICIAL MEMBER No. 4711

THE ROCKY HORROR PICTURE SHOW OFFICIAL FAN CLUB

EXCLUSIVE MEMBERS RECEIVE:

1) RARE ROCKY HORROR PHOTOS

2) Officially numbered MEMBERSHIP CARD.

3) RHPS GREETING CARDS AND MAGAZINES

4) FULL-COLOR POSTERS, from The Rocky Horror Picture Show

5) THE TRANSYLVANIAN — an introductory issue of our fan club publication.

6) INFORMATION — How to write your favorite Rocky Horror star.

7) DANCE INSTRUCTIONS to the TIME WARP.

DON'T DREAM IT. JOIN IT.

For a New Membership, Please Send $9.95 plus $1.00 postage.
FOREIGN FANS: $13.00 in U.S. funds only.

THE ROCKY HORROR PICTURE SHOW
OFFICIAL FAN CLUB
204 West 20th Street
New York City, New York 10011

Official licensee of
REP #

NAME: _____
ADDRESS: _____
CITY/STATE: _____
ZIP/COUNTRY: _____
FAVORITE STAR: _____
NAME & LOCATION OF YOUR RHPS THEATER: _____

SAL PIRO, President

◄ FAN CLUB LEAFLET

TRANSYLVANIAN MAGAZINE COVER

- Richard O'Brien 'SHOCK TREATMENT'
- STAR UPDATES
- FAN CLUB NEWS

For over a decade now the film has been Sal's life, his mainstay and his reason for being. When he ambles into the packed auditorium wearing an outrageous wig and the look of a benevolent teddy bear the celebrants greet him with rapture. He speaks and they make an exhilarated response. As in an age-old litany, the dialogue between priest and worshippers is made up of chants known by heart and sanctified by long usage. The seats are filled with characters wearing basque and fishnet stockings, bald-headed hunchbacks, donnish persons in velvet stock and diamond tie-pin, girls in Anne Miller costume and top hat, and fair-haired youths in golden briefs. Preening himself in a corner is a fan got up as an enormous pair of voluptuous lips.

one of the sickies

Sal's sister Lillias, whom he describes as 'New York's best Magenta', has seen the film almost as many times as he has. 'I've been with the picture since the very beginning,' he says. 'I'm one of the sickies who started the audience participation. I was a little older than most of the others, so I sort of became the leader.' His mother came to the tenth anniversary birthday party at which he presided in Manhattan. A journalist asked if she ever told him to grow up. 'No,' he replied firmly. 'She *knows* I'm grown up.'

A twenty-three-year-old fan who has witnessed more than fifty showings since 1978, often dressed as Dr Frank'n'Furter, explains: 'It's funny, but it's also very sad. Most people miss the sadness. Part of the picture's attraction is that it's truly bizarre, something audiences can't experience any place else.' The picture became a social event for him and his friends. They would dress up, dine at a restaurant and then go to the cinema. It was an excuse for them to get together. They never, though, disrupted the film with overexuberance. 'It was more like making responses in church,' he says.

This decorum is the result of Sal's behaviour as a master of ceremonies who controls the fans' ebullience with kindly firmness. He is like the father of a noisy group of children, anxious for them to have a good time but careful, nonethless, to ensure that all does not end in tears. At midnight on Fridays and Saturdays the scenes in the Eighth Street Playhouse, New York, where the film took up permanent residence, are duplicated in San Francisco and Pittsburgh, in Hermosa Beach and New Orleans, in Chicago and Petaluna, in Austin and Berkeley, and right across the United States of America. Sometimes, before the film is screened, fans put on a half-hour revue of their own. On other occasions they sing and dance in a fully lit auditorium while the movie unrolls regardless. At the Sena Mall in New Orleans the hundredth screening was marked by the presentation of a huge many-tiered wedding cake. With it came an ample bouquet of red roses and a gigantic pair of red lips.

sing, bitch!

Historians reckon that the custom of talking back to the screen with alternative dialogue originated in 1976. In that year a schoolteacher called Louis F. Farese Jr saw the picture for the first time. He went to see it again and found himself, involuntarily, making audible comments. As Brad and Janet stumbled through the rain while Frank's castle lowered in the dark, he suddenly called out: 'Buy an umbrella!' This, with a few added refinements, is now enshrined in the official talk-back as: 'Buy an umbrella, you cheap bitch . . . Sing, bitch!' No exact date can be ascertained for the time when people started dressing up. All that matters is that they did.

At midnight sessions there are queues outside the cinema. Once the doors open the auditorium quickly fills up with 'virgins' who are seeing it for the first time, 'regulars' who can boast of more than fifteen viewings, and 'veterans' who in full dress provide the floor show. Sal Piroa calls majestically for silence and leads a deafening Tim Curry cheer, 'C-U-R-R-Y'. He announces forthcoming events, reads out messages received, and names, amid loud applause, those present who have reached their 200th viewing. Virgins are offered a welcome and some of the luckier ones are awarded a greetings card three feet long specially designed by Sal to incorporate a ribald symbol.

The floor show begins with clones of Frank, Brad, Janet and Riff-Raff scampering around and mimicking the screen originals. Some of them have become well known in their own right. They stage revues and go on tours of cinemas. A girl who often portrays Frank is fascinated by the challenge of acting a man acting a woman. 'The one thing I wanted was to get to the point where people would not be sure which I was,' she has said. 'I am intrigued by the fact that there is a masculine element in me, and I enjoy being able to bring it out. Women's lib aside, we still believe feminity is soft and passive. As Frank, I have a chance to be on top of things, to be a faggot Clint Eastwood. Frank'n'Furter may wear Joan Crawford make-up and high heels, but he's still so masculine there's no way you could mistake him for a woman.'

On Sunday, 20 February 1978, the first Convention of Rocky fans was held on Long Island. They were promised a sight of their idols in the flesh, a question-and-answer session, a masquerade in which the stars of the film would be judges, a special turn by Meatloaf, and, of course, a celebration screening. John Mandracchia, one of the organizers, telephoned Richard O'Brien in London. He was astonished. 'What kind of convention would that be?' the latter enquired incredulously. Like everyone else, he had assumed that the film was as unsuccessful in America as it had been in England, and news of its triumphant revival had not yet crossed the Atlantic. With the other stars he flew over for the occasion and emerged from Customs staggering under the weight of a large trunk which bore the legend 'Richard O'Brien' inscribed all over it. The trunk was heavy, he could carry it no longer, and he dropped it with a resounding thud on Mandracchia's foot.

Although he walked for some time after with a limp, Mandraccia had the pleasure of knowing that the convention was a success. Richard O'Brien was joined by Pat Quinn and Little Nell in an exuberant performance of the 'Time Warp'. Little Nell, despite laryngitis, sang determinedly to roars of applause from the crowded audience. Meatloaf, too, had laryngitis and found himself unable to croak 'Hot Patootie'. Richard sprang on the stage, belted out his own version and brought the house down.

MEATLOAF IS EDDIE

A Texan born and raised in Dallas, Meatloaf played in the Broadway and road show production of "Hair," off-Broadway in "Rainbow" and "Silver Queen" and in Joseph Papp's Royal Shakespeare Festival presentations of "As You Like It" and "More Than You Deserve." He has made records for RSO and Motown, where he recorded the hit song "What You See Is What You Get."

Meatloaf was a member of the Los Angeles and New York companies of "The Rocky Horror Show," and now he recreates the role of Eddie in the screen version, "The Rocky Horror Picture Show."

the Curry cheer

The convention had been so popular that another was held before the end of the year in October. All tickets were quickly sold and hundreds of would-be spectators queued up outside for standing room only. 'Who do you want?' coyly enquired the master of ceremonies. 'Tim Curry!' bellowed the close-packed ranks of fans. 'Who?' he asked innocently. 'TIM CURRY!' they screamed again. 'Then here he is, ladies and gentlemen.' The curtains swung open to reveal the elegant Mr Curry, not in the garb of Dr Frank but wearing the restrained casual clothes of private life. Any disappointment at his modest shirt and corduroys was swept away by delight in the star's presence. His charm and suavity proved as seductive as his flamboyance in the notorious role he turned into

his own. The evening erupted again when Jonathan Adams made an all-conquering entry as Dr Scott in his wheelchair to carol his lament for nephew Eddie:

> When Eddie said he didn't like his Teddy,
> You knew he was a no-good-kid.
> But when he threatened your life with a Switch blade knife.
> What a guy.
> Makes you cry.
> And I did . . .

Seven years later, in 1985, the film's tenth anniversary called for celebrations. These took the shape of a Halloween Night on 31 October at the Beacon Theatre in New York. Richard O'Brien came, and so did Little Nell and Jonathan Adams. Doors opened at 6.30 and a live show began at 8.30. There were free gifts for lucky ones, a competition for the best costume, live numbers performed by the most accomplished look-alikes, and, the advance notice promised mysteriously, a 'surprise'. Aficionados who had seen the film countless times debated finer points of research with the earnestness that inspired those mediaeval disputants seeking to establish the precise number of angels who could dance on the end of a needle. Where, for example, was the town of Denton, home of Brad and Janet? Careful study of the atlas revealed several towns of that name, although informed opinion leaned to Kentucky. In that state, goes the ingenious argument, may be found the townships of Frankfort (Frank), Columbia, Bradfordsville (Brad), Scottsville (Dr Scott) and Eddieville (Eddie). Other casuists limited themselves to crucial problems of editing. They pointed out that although the Narrator mentioned late November as the time of the incident, President Nixon's resignation speech which is played over on Brad's car radio took place in August. Continuity presented another rich field for discussion. How many people had noticed, they enquired excitedly, that Christopher Biggins, as a Transylvanian, handed over a tray of cakes only to be shown holding it again in a subsequent shot?

Presiding, as always, with good humour and imperturbability was Sal Piro. For a decade he had been co-ordinating fans' activities not only in New York but throughout the whole country, travelling, exhorting, advising. Among the goodies he had distributed were the famous Little Nell fan kit and the Tim Curry 'fearless' T-shirt. History was to be in his debt for the audience participation album which constituted a record of the classic performance at the Eighth Street Playhouse

THE SECOND OFFICIAL ROCKY HORROR CONVENTION PROGRAM $1.00

TONIGHT, IS THE NIGHT YOU'RE GOING TO REMEMBER FOR A VERY LONG TIME

★ THIS PROGRAM INCLUDES ★
- CONVENTION SCHEDULE
- SPECIAL PHOTO'S FROM LAST CONVENTION
- PLUS MORE - ALSO FOR YOUR enter-tainment music to listen to BY FRESH AIRE

SECOND CONVENTION PROGRAMME

with Sal delivering his celebrated warm-up and the audience responding vigorously. He himself, in the live show that accompanied the screening, had dashed on stage to sing 'touch-a-touch-touch-a-toucha-me' dressed in Janet's bra and knickers, black hair sprouting between the lace.

Innumerable had been the quizzes he devised. What colour was the Transylvanian flag? Did Brad ever put the ring on Janet's finger? Who was the priest in the wedding scene? On which leg did Frank wear his ankle bracelet? How many times did Riff-Raff and Magenta perform the Transylvanian greeting? How many rings did Eddie wear? What type of car did Brad drive? He was a master of trivia, a virtuoso of the unconsidered detail.

He has been written about in papers that range from *Time* to *Rolling Stone*. On primetime television he was interviewed propounding the gospel of Rocky as he had once propounded the gospel of the Bible to his scripture classes. Scrapbooks, articles, magazines and introductions flowed from his ready typewriter to be snapped up by 20,000 club members throughout the USA and even further afield. At colleges and other places of education he lectured on the phenomenon of which he was a part. Innumerable commentaries and exegetical writings poured out from his headquarters in West 20th Street, New York City, to enlighten the faithful. Filmmakers acknowledged his authority and used his services in *Fame* and in *Shock Treatment*, the Richard O'Brien production that followed on the adventures of Frank. Between assignments he even found time to devise and write a novel line in comic greetings cards.

In the spring of 1986, however, a malaise descended on the activities of the club. Intending fans received, in reply to their enquiries, a back-number of the club's magazine *The Transylvanian* and a selection of other small items. The accompanying letter warned that the advertisements for various Rocky merchandise carried in the magazine were invalid. It went on to explain that the success of the tenth anniversary Halloween had inspired ambitions to expand the club. New ideas for material to be distributed had been suggested to the company that made the film. But, the letter continued, there were 'some serious problems'. Legal difficulties were mentioned. The tone cheered up a little with an announcement that everyone who had applied would be officially registered as a charter member and receive a free button, membership card and updated newsletter.

An elegiac phrase about 'the loss' of people at the studio who had been involved

TENTH ANNIVERSARY ANNOUNCEMENT

with the fan club concealed drama. At about this time the film company was taken over as part of a massive package deal by Rupert Murdoch's vast communications business. Either before or after this event Tim Deegan, by now Vice-President (advertising), after marketing the film in the early years with flair and enterprise, abruptly departed from the scene. Circumstances decreed that all projects associated with him should float for a time in limbo. No one knows what the future of the club will be. For the time being all the posters, the badges, the 'Time Warp' instruction sheets, the trivia questionnaires and the greetings cards are items of historic interest, slowly gathering in value until, say thirty years hence, they appear in auction rooms to be fought over at high prices by collectors. Or in the legendary John Kobal collection.

where are they now?

Frank speaking

On an April morning in 1973 Richard O'Brien happened to be walking down a London street and caught sight of a friend. It was Tim Curry, an actor with whom he had recently toured in *Hair*. They exchanged their news and Curry asked what Richard was doing at the moment. He was, he replied, on the lookout for a 'strong man' who could sing as well as act, and he had just called at a nearby gymnasium in the hope of discovering such. At that moment Curry was appearing in a play by Barry Reckord called *Give the Gaffers Time to Love You* at The Theatre Upstairs. Richard explained that the next play there was to be his own *Rocky Horror Show*. Would he like to audition for it?

Tim was intrigued by what he heard. At this audition for Jim Sharman he sang 'Tutti Frutti', a Little Richard number, and spoke a few passages of dialogue. He was engaged on the spot, not as Rocky but as Dr Frank-'n'Furter. The role enchanted him. It was entirely different from anything he had done before and that, chiefly, is why he was so pleased with it. 'It takes a certain amount of courage to play Frank,' he said, referring among other matters to the exiguous dress of basque, stockings and high heels. 'But the only thing I'm sure about as a performer is that you have to be dangerous. If you're going to take a risk, take a big one. It's like the circus. You're on a tightrope, and the people come to watch you fall. If you fall with your whole heart, then that's all right. You have to be as brave as you can in your work. Give as much blood as you can.'

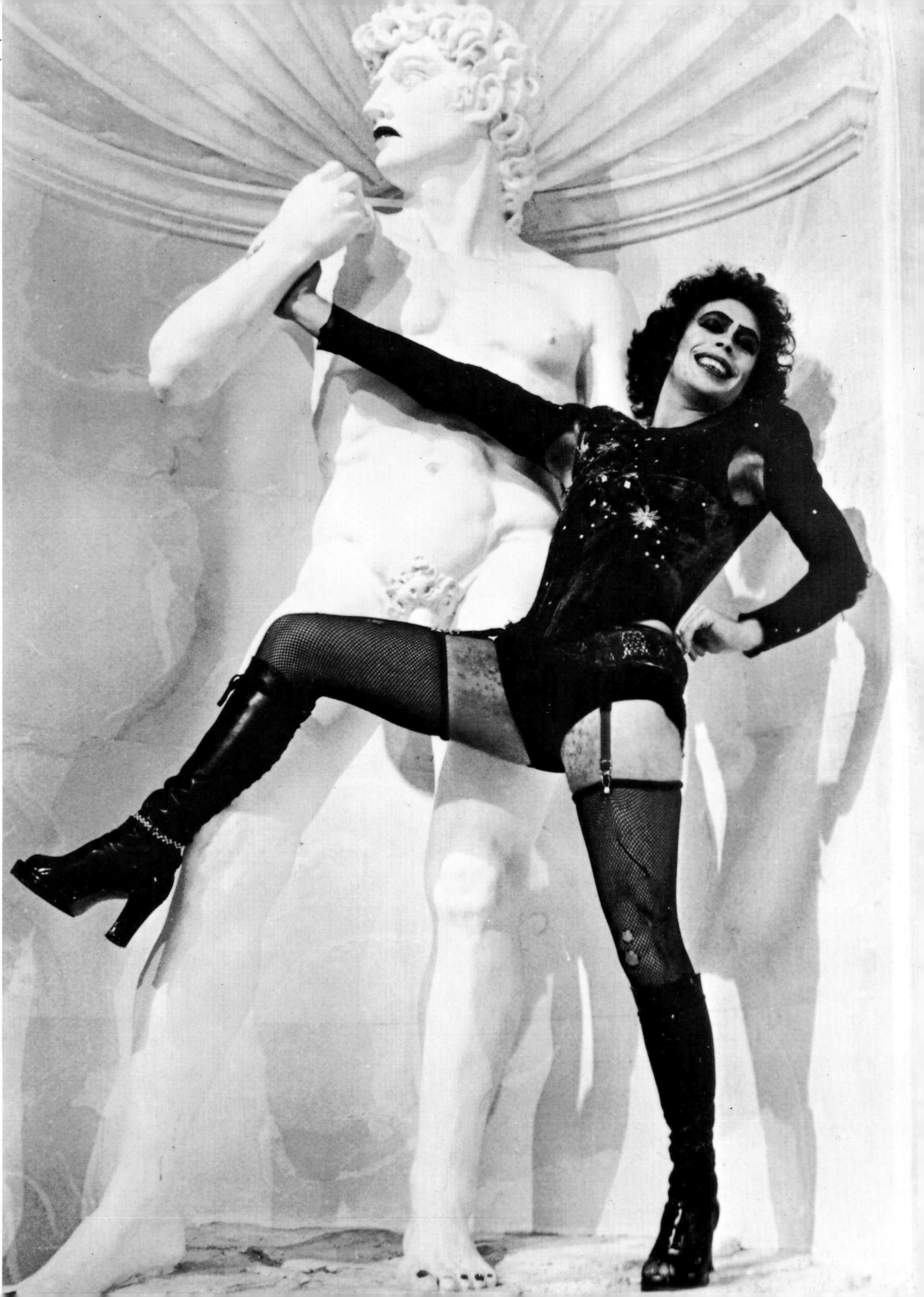

TIM CURRY AS DR FRANK'N'FURTER (1973)

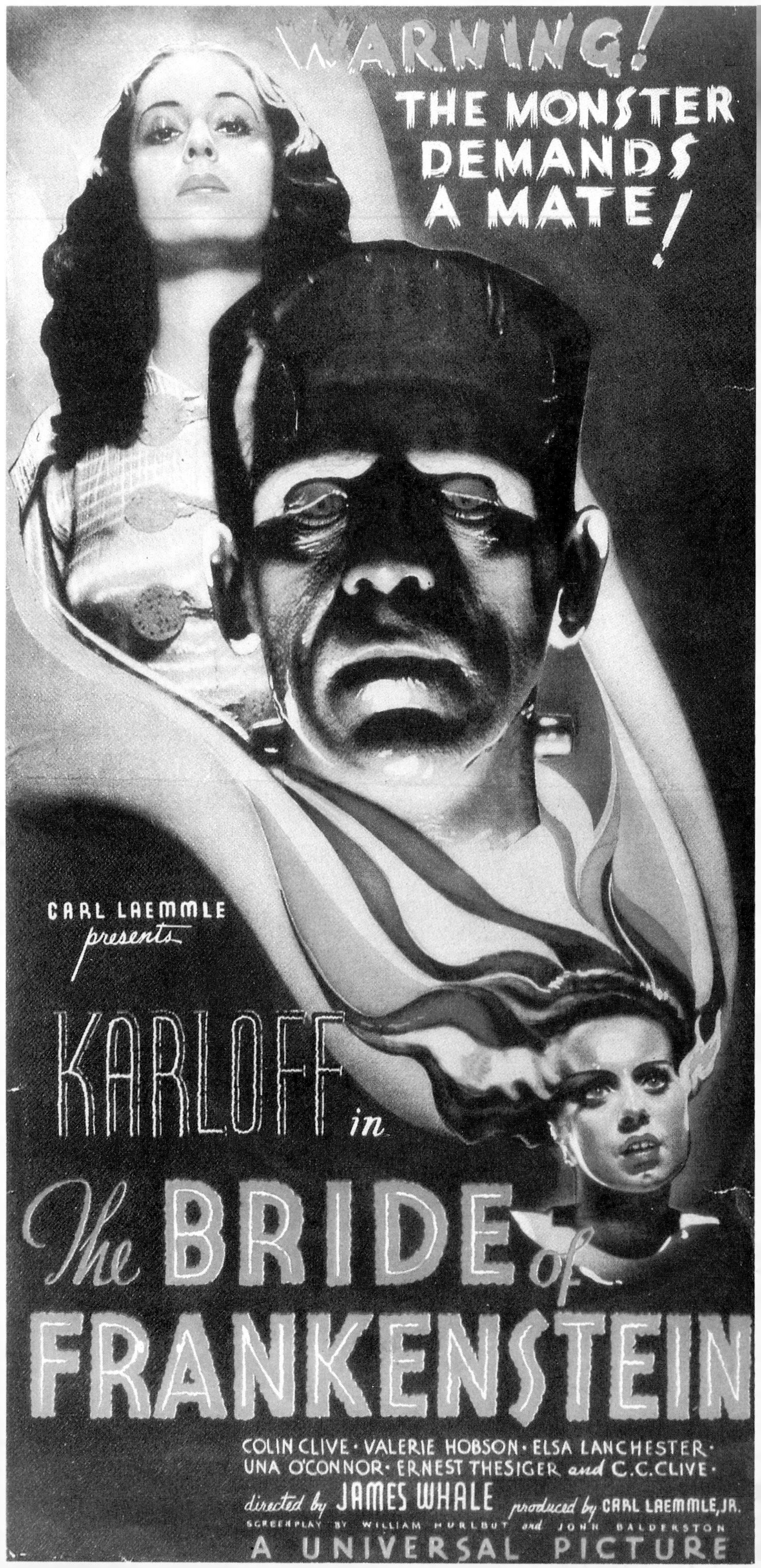
WARNING!
THE MONSTER
DEMANDS
A MATE!
CARL LAEMMLE
presents
KARLOFF in
The BRIDE of
FRANKENSTEIN
COLIN CLIVE · VALERIE HOBSON · ELSA LANCHESTER ·
UNA O'CONNOR · ERNEST THESIGER and C.C. CLIVE ·
directed by JAMES WHALE produced by CARL LAEMMLE, JR.
SCREENPLAY BY WILLIAM HURLBUT and JOHN BALDERSTON
A UNIVERSAL PICTURE

the Transylvanian accent

First came the make-up. Originally his hair was dyed blue, although after a while he decided to let it grow out and revert to a natural black. His features were, in any case, a gift, with the big wide eyes, the arched brows, the delicately shaped nose, the dramatic lips and the broad defiant chin. The accent he should choose for Frank was a problem. He started off in mock Translyvanian. This did not seem to work so he switched to American. Then Jim Sharman suggested an English accent and everything fell into place. The sort of shoes he needed presented difficulty. Shoes were very important, and it was only at quite a late stage in rehearsals that he got them right. The question was one of balance and dynamics, and for that reason he worked from the feet upwards. When, for example, he played the part of a soldier he had always found boots to be crucial. Once Dr Frank's diamanté high heels had been settled on he felt at ease. The elements of his all-important first entrance were complete, and an indication of his success is that, when he bounded on the stage, quite a few men in the audience turned their heads away with embarrassment. There had, up to 1973, been no real tradition of male exhibitionism or male eroticism. Dr Frank helped to create it.

The Royal Court was familiar ground to Curry. He had already played there in four productions including the Barry Reckord piece mentioned above, *The Sport of My Mad Mother, Man Is Man* and *The Baby Elephant.* For over a year he toured in *Hair* and, as proof of his versatility, also sang the role of Puck, in Britten's opera *A Midsummer Night's Dream.* The part of Dr Frank'n'Furter, he told an interviewer, seemed to be a coming together of all the things he did best.

TIM CURRY MAKES UP

Rehearsals with Jim Sharman were enjoyable. He somehow created, says Curry, the sort of atmosphere in which nine strong personalities could work together without discord. They would start at 11.00 a.m. with coffee and sing old standards like 'Donna' from *Hair* to get in the mood. There was a strong corporate feeling and everyone was wholeheartedly committed to the project. 'It's the sort of show I feel is always with me during the day,' he said when *Rocky* had settled in its permanent home at the Chelsea cinema, 'and I get the strongest feeling of *working up* to a performance I've ever had.'

He comes from Cheshire where he was born on 19 April 1946. His father, a Methodist chaplain in the Navy, happened to be stationed there at the time, and only an accident of birth made Tim a North-countryman. In any case, a few months later came a posting to Hong Kong, and, three years afterwards, yet another move. Tim's father met his mother in Malta. They were married in Egypt, and his sister was born there. He himself was conceived in South Africa and born in England. Such incessant travelling, he thinks, was an ideal upbringing for an actor because he never stayed in one place long enough to make permanent friends and had to learn how to please other children very quickly.

When the boy was twelve his father died and the family settled in London. After school Tim went to Birmingham University and came away with a combined honours degree in English and Drama. The young graduate had long since decided on an actor's career. An actor, he reasoned, can pretend to be someone else by virtue of using whatever part of himself he understands enough to project.

The fifteen months he spent in the touring company of *Hair* was, he says, almost like doing National Service and much more valuable. 'It was my first job. I had two lines and jumped up and down in the back. I did whatever part anyone else was too stoned to play.'

For another six months he worked at the Glasgow Citizens' Theatre with eighteen other people all under the age of thirty. 'The actors were encouraged to be magical,' he says, 'whereas the English tradition is very literary and technical. We just went out there and bit off great chunks. It should have been laughable, yet no one laughed. We began to learn what wave we were operating on. We learned that theatre is intangible.'

eighteen pounds a week

After Glasgow came a tour with the Scottish Opera Company and several small roles in London productions. By 1973, date of *The Rocky Horror Show*, he had appeared five times at the Royal Court, a theatre where he felt very much at home. 'But you almost have to pay them to work there,' he said at the time. 'I earned £18 a week at The Theatre Upstairs and at the time *Rocky* came up I had an overdraft of £350 and the offer of a better-paying television part, which I turned down.'

He has, throughout his career, always been ready to make daring choices. 'If you're an actor, you have to make choices more often than other people. Your life and work are more intertwined. So I live for what I am doing now, and tomorrow I'll do something else. When I choose what I do, and how I do it, I'd just like to be brave — make fewer compromises . . . I just want to be able to change all the time.'

Lord of darkness

Back at Drury Lane his interpretation of the Pirate King in *The Pirates of Penzance,* a Michael White production, gained him the Variety Club Award as Best Stage Actor. Living nomadically between London, Los Angeles and New York, he also made a number of films. In *Annie* he co-starred as Rooster with Albert Finney, and in *Clue* he acted an impeccable English butler caught up by a farcical who-dunnit based on the board game Cluedo. His nearest approach, in bravura terms that is, to Dr Frank was his performance as the Lord of Darkness in *Legend*. Here, as the devil himself fitted out with a stentorian bull-like roar, he impersonated an eight-foot-high monster, fanged, horned and cloven-hoofed. The elaborate make-up took seven hours to create, and, so

intense was the strain of wearing the costume, he could only work two days a week, and even then had to be fed on draughts of oxygen. 'I look like two hundred pounds of condemned Tandoori,' he said ruefully on this occasion. 'They weren't too careful taking the make-up off at first and I got blisters on my back and face. I fell over once wearing all the gear. There was a hell of crash.' But, again, as with Dr Frank, he refused to be type-cast. 'There are some roles where you have to get by on sheer force of personality, but I don't want to be known as a tack merchant who goes around endangering the scenery.'

There have also been a number of television plays. But it is in the theatre that he finds the widest scope for his versatile talent. On the stage each performance is different. The actor can sculpt and mould his presentation according to the reaction from his audience, which is, quite as much as him, a vital element in the act of creation. An audience can inspire new intonations, new gestures, new ways of delivering a speech. It can sometimes, through its attitude, bring about an entirely fresh reading of a part which otherwise might not have emerged. This is why stage actors treasure the contact with living spectators which film and television cannot give.

Recently the National Theatre has provided the setting of Curry's most brilliant achievements. As a deliberate reaction against his role of the Pirate King in *The Pirates of Penzance,* all glitter and swashbuckling glamour, he chose to play Bob Acres in their production of Sheridan's classic comedy *The Rivals*. In order to portray this amiable character he put on extra weight, two stones of it, and created an endearing image of good nature and optimism, beaming, careless, youthfully uncritical. No one seeing this likeable body amble round the stage would have associated him with the weird Dr Frank'n'Furter.

SOME OF THE SHOW'S ORIGINAL 1973 CAST

RICHARD O'BRIEN LIMBERS UP IN HIS DRESSING ROOM

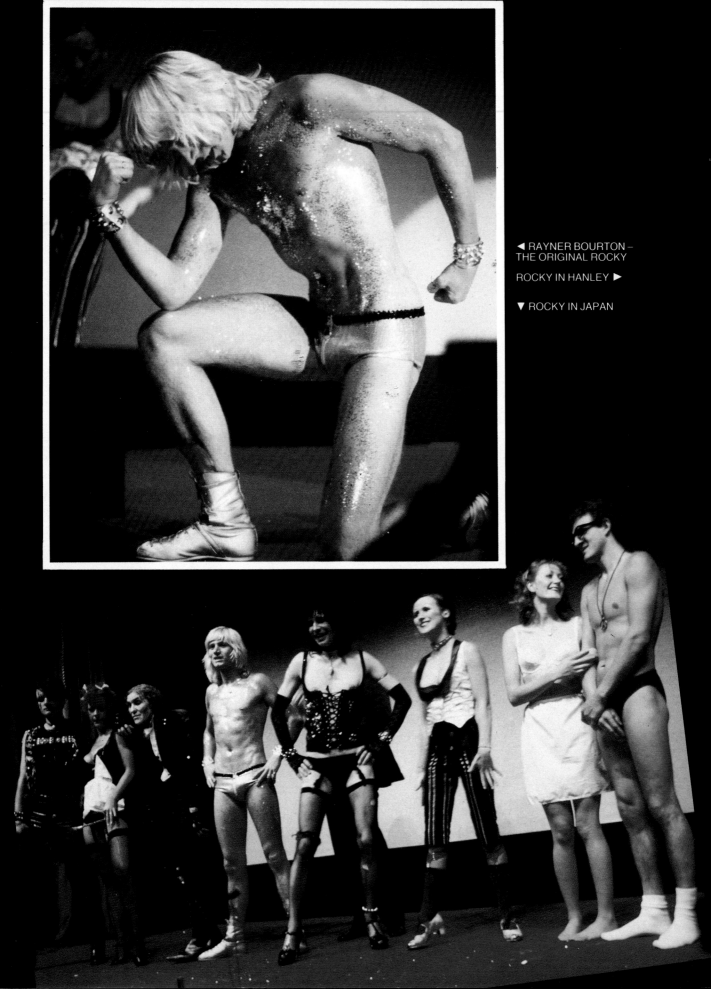

◄ RAYNER BOURTON –
THE ORIGINAL ROCKY

ROCKY IN HANLEY ►

▼ ROCKY IN JAPAN

DAVID IAN
AS
ROCKY

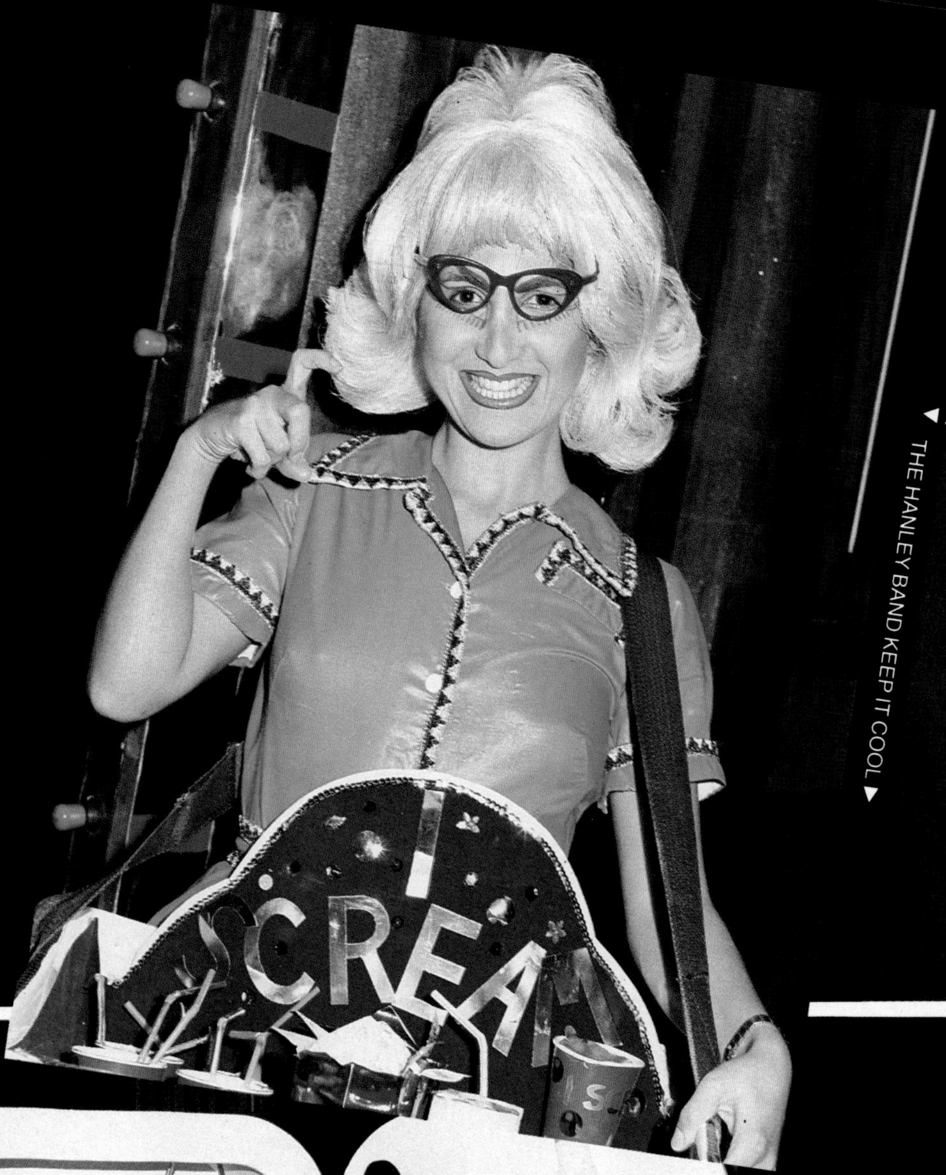

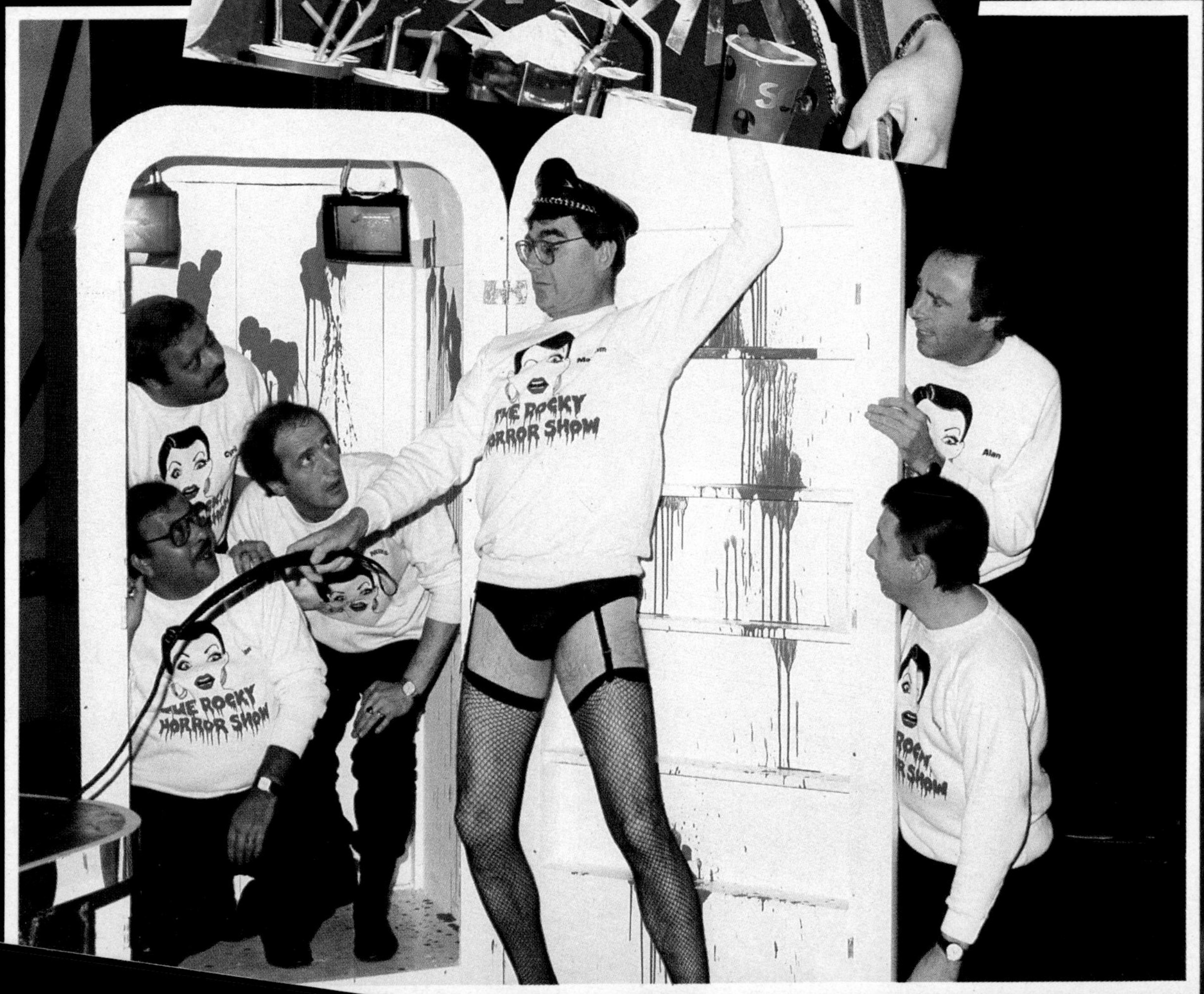

◄ ADEEN FOGLE USHERETTES

THE HANLEY BAND KEEP IT COOL ►

RIFF RAFF WITH LAZERS ▼   RIFF RAFF WITH FRIENDS ▶

A CLIMAX AT LEICESTER . . .

AND A GRAND FINALE

read my lips

His protean gift spills over into music as well. A few years after *The Rocky Horror Show* he brought out three record albums. The first of these, 'Read My Lips', was successful and encouraged him to make a second, 'Fearless', for which he wrote six of the lyrics and some of the music for the nine songs. In 1979 he went on an American tour with his own backing group. The attraction of recording songs and then singing them live was that he could reach an audience directly without having to express himself through the medium of character. There was no longer the barrier of a script between himself and the people he wanted to get at.

Despite a third album entitled 'Simplicity' in 1980 he has, in the years that followed, concentrated on his acting career except for a period as host of 'Saturday Night Live' on American television. Soon after his role as Dr Frank'n'Furter he played the Dadaist poet Tristan Tzara in Tom Stoppard's *Travesties*. This was for a production on Broadway where Curry also took the leading role of Mozart in Peter Shaffer's *Amadeus* and won a nomination for the Tony Award as best actor.

TIM CURRY (FRANK) ▶

♣ THE ♣ ROCKY ♣ HORROR SHOW ♣

pig-faced tattle

The 1985-86 season at the National Theatre was something of an *annus mirabilis* for Curry. He began it as the mischief-making fop Tattle in Congreve's *Love for Love*. Inevitably comparisons were made with Laurence Olivier's authoritative version of the role twenty years previously, though none were unfavourable to Curry. Tattle threads his devious way in a world of cruelty, lies and intrigue not without moments of Hogarthian unroariousness, as when, caught out in an unsuccessful attempt at seduction, he is obliged to flee through a garden and to pose stock-still as a rustic ornament. Pig-faced and untrustworthy, Curry's Tattle represented malice incarnate. You knew that, if you'd been foolish enough to confide in him, he would immediately, and with gleeful spite, have trumpeted the news far and wide throughout a decadent society of which he was the most decadent member. 'One of the hardest but most enjoyable things about playing Tattle,' Curry observes, 'is to remember that he doesn't understand what people think of him, and doesn't realize when they are winding him up.'

Next came his role as the gangster Macheath in Brecht's *The Threepenny Opera* to Weill's acrid music. The first number was performed against a poster bearing a picture of the wanted man. It climaxed with Macheath slashing a hole from behind and making a sensational entry. Although the production was full of ingenious touches like this, Curry dominated all with his vicious little moustache, his black hair smoothed flat over

his head like patent leather, his pointed white teeth glistening like a shark's. In moments of excitement, as during the rooftop chase, he was muscular and athletic. In the quieter scenes he implied unfathomable reserves of danger and villainy.

Being identified with a single character is something he has always, and successfully, tried to avoid. Throughout his whole career he has deliberately refrained from imposing any sort of pattern on it.

Once a challenge has been met and dealt with he is eager to pass on to other things. He had, for example, always been determined that at the age of forty he wouldn't turn round and say 'I could have been a singer'. So, characteristically, he took a year or so off from his activities on stage, film and television to make his name as a rock singer. He looks back on the period with a measure of satisfaction. 'I was very serious about it and did it very thoroughly. I even wrote most of the last two records. But in the end I didn't like the people very much, and I didn't like the way the word "product" rules the business. Also the kind of attention and following I had was not a very comfortable thing. People going through your rubbish, and knocking on your door at 3 a.m. Death threats. Horrible.' Still, he had done what he wanted to do, just as he had wanted to do all the other things in his life. It was, he concedes, valuable because one discipline nourishes and informs another.

Like many other people, he was astonished by the success of *The Rocky Horror Show*. He had never expected to find himself involved in an experimental production which would flourish and grow until it had become a phenomenon comparable to *Hair*, and, as a film, to *Gone With The Wind*. Long after he had left the show it prospered and continues to attract new cultists as the years go by. Again and again, when you look at the potted biographies of young actors in London theatre programmes, you find that they have played the obligatory stint of Dr Frank'n'Furter in touring productions. It has become a badge of honour, a sign of graduation, a rite of passage.

It is true that, being an actor of many gifts, he would in any case have won distinction sooner or later. Circumstance dictated that he was to do so in the role of Dr Frank. Yet the true artist is one who is never satisfied and who is constantly searching to renew himself. Frank, although a creature of endless, glittering bravura, has long ago been, in Curry's word, 'amputated' to make room for the development of other characters. The actor who brought him to life on stage is eager for new adventures.

with a view to a tomb

Upon a signboard that hangs over the porch you may read, in impeccable Gothic characters, the legend: TOMB VIEW. It designates a neat little Victorian terrace house with a rambling garden that enjoys a prospect of the most commodious cemetery in North London. Is it by chance or design, you wonder, that the next turning up the street should be called Exit Road?

The place is most suitably approached when a storm is gathering, when clouds black and pendulous hover in the sky. Fat raindrops begin to fall. Lightning flickers and casts a lurid gleam on the signboard TOMB VIEW as it creaks and quivers in the rising wind. There is no doorbell and you hopefully jiggle the flap of the letterbox which gives out a doleful clatter. As you wait you look through the bow window and see, standing in the middle of the room, a bicycle, desolate, dusty and disused.

This is the dwelling-place of Jonathan Adams, teacher, dancer, actor, composer, artist and man of many parts, including two in *The Rocky Horror Show,* for which he has played both the Narrator and Dr Scott. As the Narrator in the original stage version he gave the impression of a bulky, heavy-jowled Kissinger-like figure who entered into the rock numbers, as one critic said, 'with the stately aplomb of a dowager duchess doing a strip'. Another found him 'a velvet-jacketed Lustgarten figure who acts as the straight contrast to all those kinky jinks and narrates the show as if we were all personally responsible for the evil doings.* Everyone agreed that his greatest moment came when he imperturbably began to call the steps for 'Let's do the Time Warp Again'.

Edgar Lustgarten — a barrister noted for his broadcasts, films and television features about famous crimes, many of them narrated by himself with a piercing eye and commanding, unctuous tones.

JONATHAN ADAMS

• • • In the film he was Dr Everett Scott – 'Or should I say Dr Von Scott?' as Frank sneers when he meets his scientist rival. For Dr Scott is of German origin, according to the screenplay, and reminds one of Von Braun, the scientist-engineer who researched and perfected so many death-dealing missiles for his employer Hitler that, at the end of World War II, he entered the pay of America and carried on similar work for the Pentagon. His was too valuable a brain to be wasted. One of the joys of Dr Scott in the film is his Americo-Teutonic accent, a plummy tone beautifully sustained by the actor who also, in his big number 'Eddie's Teddy', displays a rich bass voice that swoons to velvety depths on the line 'He left home the day she died'.

Once inside TOMB VIEW you look out through sitting-room windows to an overgrown expanse with the cemetery beyond, vast, quiet, still. On pediments and shelves stand sculptures and elaborate models in clay and wickerwork. The walls are clustered with Jonathan Adams' pictures, all of them in immaculate frames. The bicycle in the front room, explains the master of the house, has stood there for the past five years because the tyres are flat and he has not yet contrived to pump them up again.

He was once an art master in his native Northampton, having trained as a painter at Chelsea Art School and London University. During his National Service he administered pills, potions and swabs in the RAF Medical Corps. Then he went, as the saying goes, into teaching and for five long years wrestled to instil notions of perspective and fine art in the minds of reluctant small boys. A refugee from the blackboard jungle, he turned to acting and promptly learned a great deal about the art of resting. As a member of the Northampton Repertory Theatre for three years he played many roles that extended from Shakespeare to Agatha Christie. To each of them he brought a certain haunted quality that remained with him from his classroom experiences.

The monasticism of a repertory life began to pall and he fled, as he had fled from teaching, this time to London. There he worked with the Children's Theatre Company and at Sadler's Wells. For two years he played in the long-running *Alibi for a Judge* at the Savoy and, from time to time, featured in music-hall productions at the Players' Theatre underneath the arches by Charing Cross. He also made television films. His rueful features have decorated the home screen in serials like *Triton* and *Pegasus*. More recently he shaved off the beard he usually wears between acting engagements for a cameo role in Jeffrey Archer's *First*

5JONATHAN ADAMS AS THE NARRATOR PRESIDES OVER THE TIME WARP▶

Among Equals, a brooding, Callaghan-type part. It saddens him that, to date, *TV Times* have not asked to do an article about his house and garden, a riot of wild profusion that would be perfect as the setting for Frances Hodgson Burnett's *The Secret Garden*. Secret it most assuredly is, for it looks as if no human foot can have been set there for generations.

Jonathan Adams is as much an artist as he is an actor. In youth he was very taken with Dadaism, the art movement which, during the 1920s, preceded Surrealism and quickly burned itself out. It proclaimed a doctrine of incoherence and destructiveness. Words, declared the leaders of Dada, could mean anything or nothing at all and were linked together by pure chance. Dada meetings usually ended, not surprisingly, in brawls and fist fights. Another influence on Adams was the nineteenth-century poet Lautréamont whom the Surrealists honoured as a worthy precursor. His poetry, which varies from the erotic to the delirious, is marked by hallucinatory visions peopled with toads, vampires, octopuses and terrifying creatures inhabiting the seashore. He speaks of nightmares drenched in blood.

landscape with dentures

On the walls of TOMB VIEW hang samples of Jonathan's art. One-man shows of his have been held in Northampton and Coventry City Art Galleries, at the South London Art Gallery and at the Arts Centre, University of London Institute of Education. Besides his collages, photomontages and oils he has created humanoid assemblages and groups that might have been conceived in Dr Frank's laboratory.

'Landscape with Dentures — The Dream of Berenice' is the title of a recent picture. You can buy it for £120. Others present variations on the theme of cathedrals — 'Cathedral among the Rocks', 'Blue Cathedral', 'Delirious Cathedral', 'Rotting Cathedral', 'Cathedral in the Jungle', 'Purple Cathedral'.

A 'Boxed Beachscape' hangs next to 'Moon Rising over Vegetation'. There are pictures of seeds blowing over a garden, of St George's Cemetery in Penang, and, nearer home, of East Finchley Cemetery which borders on the garden of TOMB VIEW. 'From time to time,' says Jonathan, 'I feel the need to escape from the imagery of my collage mindscapes and "go back to Nature" . . . at these times I like nothing so much as to trudge off into the jungle with solar topee, insect repellent, sketch book, umbrella — even oil paints, canvas and easel, just as the Impressionists used to do, and make a representation in the field.'

From these wanderings he has come back with images of a banana tree in Bali, a plantation in Penang, mountains in Albania, valleys in Turkey, a fig tree in Greece and a pool in Haiti. A carnival in Venice is abruptly succeeded by five studies of his North London garden in the snow. A cactus in the desert sits demurely beside classical studies inspired by Laocoon and Narcissus. A nude on a beach in the shade of a tree is contrasted with a swarm of bees in May and the shades of night.

Dreams, nightmares, daytime visions and subconscious fears and aspirations are the materials of his art. The oils are thickly patterned and laid on with frenetic jabs. The collages have an urgent air about them, and the models and assemblages offer a blur of shapes, angles and planes in a desperate kaleidoscope. Yet the instigator of these unsettling phenomena is himself a retiring and soft-spoken character. His clothes are unobtrusive — an open-necked shirt, a woolly cardigan, corduroy trousers — and he speaks in a low voice. He lolls on a Victorian chaise-longue and dispenses coffee procured from mysterious regions elsewhere in the house. His usual expression of melancholy lights up as he gives a vague smile at the end of each sentence. An attractive aura of disillusionment lingers around him. But, suddenly, the actor in him takes over, he is transformed, and with glinting eye and mobile features he declaims a line as he would on the stage.

JONATHAN ADAMS WITH SOME
OF HIS PAINTINGS

master and madman

The Cabinet of Dr Caligari has been an important influence on him. This old silent film masterpiece of German Expressionism tells the tale of a sleep-walking murderer controlled by an all-powerful master. The scenes are enacted against backgrounds of painted canvas, all jagged lines and zig-zags composed following the logic of a rigorous visual geometry. The sleep-walker dies of exhaustion and his master ends up as the director of a madhouse. A copy features among Jonathan's treasured collection of ancient 9.5 mm films. He also has *Faust*, another early German film with the great actor Emil Jannings, and *Siegfried*, a retelling of the old Teutonic legend without the aid of Wagner. He has picked them up at collectors' functions and in junk shops and flea markets. The 9.5 mm gauge, he says, still flourishes in France. One of his most eagerly enjoyed pleasures is to show these films of an evening on his elderly 9.5 projector.

His own more recent appearances have been in *Tom Foolery* and in *Master Class*. These two entirely different productions demonstrate, very neatly, the dual nature of his versatile talent. The first had words, music and lyrics by the American comedian Tom Lehrer with designs by Gerald Scarfe. Jonathan sang and danced with the skill he showed as Dr Scott in the film of *The Rocky Horror Show*. *Master Class*, on the other hand provided a startling contrast. It is a drama by David Pownall set in the Kremlin during the 1948 conference of the Soviet Musicians' Union. The dictator Stalin, played by Timothy West, has called in the leading Russian composers Shostakovitch and Prokofiev to debate the place of the artist in Soviet life. The result poses vital questions about art and politics that can never be satisfactorily answered. As the cultural minister, Zhdanov, Jonathan created a powerful, menacing presence. There was nothing to remind you of the Narrator's comic urbanity or of Dr Scott's uneasy joviality. This was a wholly sinister figure who, in despair at ever getting artists to follow the party line, grumbled: 'Let's move the whole thing to Siberia.'

Within the muted atmosphere of TOMB VIEW the shades of Dr Scott, the Narrator and Zhdanov mingle with Dr Caligari. They produce a rich brew to nourish the creative imagination of an artist who can, as the whim takes him, translate his fantasies into paint or act them out on stage. One of the composers whose music Jonathan enjoys is that quaint character Erik Satie, bowler-hatted friend of the Surrealists and enemy of all convention. On a wall near the flat where Satie lived an unknown hand once wrote: 'This place is haunted.' Instinctively you look to see if anyone has yet inscribed such a graffito on TOMB VIEW.

JONATHAN ADAMS AT HOME

the Nell file

Once upon a time in Sydney there lived a young girl called Laura Campbell. Her father was a journalist who wrote a column for the *Sydney Telegraph*. The charm of being a journalist or indeed a writer of any kind is that you find your 'copy' all around you, and Mr Campbell needed to look no further for the material with which to fill his column than the misadventures of his family which included a quartet of four lively daughters. In his column he gave them pseudonyms, and the one he chose for Laura was 'Little Nell', a name he took from the heroine of Charles Dickens's novel *The Old Curiosity Shop*. That is how she has been known ever since.

As she grew up she revealed a talent for swimming, dancing and singing. In 1972 she represented Australia as a swimmer in the Olympic Games at Munich. This is doubtless why one of the favourite songs in her repertoire is 'The Swim', a number written by Brian Thomson who also designed *The Rocky Horror Show*. Wearing a flamboyant red bathing costume she sings it with extra special energy and has recorded at least three different versions of it. A reviewer described it as 'an attempt to shatter all the stereo tweeters in the kingdom on first playing'. She wouldn't disagree. 'My frequency is all my own,' she concedes. 'Dogs pick me up. You know, it's like the sound of breaking glass.'

When she was seventeen years old she left Sydney and came to London. Here she earned a living as a waitress and, more often, busking in the streets. Her number consisted of singing 1930s' songs and tap-dancing in top hat and tails on the pavements. One day as she was performing to queues outside the Palace Theatre waiting to see *Jesus Christ Superstar* she was spotted by the director Jim Sharman. He was then casting *The Rocky Horror Show* and instantly offered her a part as Columbia the Groupie.

Her first big moment in *The Rocky Horror Show* came during the 'Time Warp'. She contributed:

Well I was walking down the street
Just having a think
When a snake of a guy gave me an evil wink
Well it shook me up, it took me by surprise
He had a pick-up truck and the devil's eyes
Oh – he stared at me and I felt a change
Time meant nothing – never would again.

Whereupon, flourishing her sequinned top hat and flashing her spangled costume, she launched into an Ann Miller tap routine of the sort she'd been up to then diverting passers-by with in Shaftesbury Avenue. It worked beautifully.

Another of her important solos came in 'Eddie's Teddy' when Dr Scott lamented the demise of his nephew Eddie – 'a low-down cheap little punk', as the Narrator interjected disdainfully. But Columbia had felt very differently about this Elvis Presley-type figure:

Everybody shoved him
I very nearly loved him.
I said hey listen to me,
Stay sane inside insanity.
But he locked the door and threw away the key.

Like everyone else, an admiring reviewer was struck by her 'dirty, squealing laugh and a wicked pair of eyes'. He might have mentioned, too, a plump and expressive tongue which shot out and curled around her lips rather as a chameleon's tongue unreels like lightning to catch its prey and then as swiftly vanishes.

As the long run of *The Rocky Horror Show* went on she was to be succeeded by others in the part, but she had made it so much her own that her naughty little-girl gestures and teasing giggle were for ever to be associated with it. The role of Columbia launched her on a career in theatre, film and

recording studios. Afterwards she played a nymphomaniac in Derek Jarman's punk film *Jubilee* which also featured Richard O'Brien. She acted with him again in *Mickey Mouse Now* in which she appeared as a blowzy Minnie Mouse. Later, with Tim Curry, came the television series *Rock Follies* where she dyed her hair blonde and took the role of a dotty secretary.

In between films she went back home to Australia. For two years she toured with a band that specialized in the 1930s' tunes she had sung in the London streets. She interviewed people on television and, like her father before her, wrote a column. It was called the Nell File. In 1985 she visited New York on a fortnight's holiday. She has stayed there ever since.

This was because she renewed acquaintance with a young man called Keith McNally. They first met in 1973 when he was a technician operating the spotlights for *The Rocky Horror Show*. Two years later, having grown out of spotlights and London, Keith travelled to New York where he worked as a busboy, a job which ranks somewhere beneath a waiter in American restaurants, rose to be a head-waiter and then found a job at Mr Chow's where his brother as barman enjoyed a reputation for the lethal cocktails he mixed. He also met Lynn Wagenknecht who is a painter and now the mother of his two young children.

In 1979 he and Lynn went to Paris and conceived the idea of a New York café-bar-restaurant-brasserie on the lines of La Coupole. On their return they bought up an old place in downtown New York, put in tubular steel chairs and a hideous pink-and-green neon clock, and christened the result 'The Odeon'. The playwright Alan Bennett, who earlier had cast McNally as a choirboy in *Forty Years On*, was one of the original investors. 'The Odeon,' he says, 'is a theatrical experience, full of wit and excitement. Just sitting there makes me feel like Proust. There are stars among the diners, of course, but the real stars are the waiters and waitresses; it's a bit like watching a play — you want to know more about the characters.'

Nell polish

Nell's reunion with Keith and his wife inspired yet another idea: why not open a place which would be, in effect, a salon presided over by the wicked Nell herself? Since her only experience of restaurants had been as a part-time waitress in London before *The Rocky Horror Show* brought her fame, Keith trained her for a while at the Odeon.

For the new site he deliberately chose an area then noted for its downright sleaze in 14th street between 8th and 9th Avenue. The building was an old electronics shop warmed by a tiny heater. It had two layers of linoleum and a colony of rats that scuttled noisily behind worm-eaten skirting-boards. Walls crumbled, ceilings bulged and damp sprouted everywhere. Nell and Keith and Lynn set to work. They salvaged a whole staircase and transported a huge chandelier from Philadelphia to shed its kindly glimmer over the giant velvet sofas, armchairs and bar stools covered with brocade run up from old curtains. Some of the material came from the Salvation Army. Other treasures were dug up from junk shops and derelict buildings in Brooklyn and the Bronx. On the walls hang gilt-framed mirrors. A vast bar of solid mahogany stretches into infinity. Downstairs, where the disco music throbs softly, a thick velvet curtain leads into a back parlour furnished in whorehouse style and containing still more dropsical sofas.

Queen of the night

Nell is the queen of the night, wearing an off-the-shoulder red satin dress so tight that she hobbles when shimmering forward to greet you, hand held out dripping with heavy rings.

The dais in the upstairs room is periodically occupied by a flamenco group, or a jazz quartet, or a French singer. Later on Nell will perform, though her voice has not yet splintered the glass of the chandelier. While her guests guzzle pizzas and caviar, background tapes discourse soul music and salsa and tangos and jazz and Gilbert and Sullivan.

On opening night, of course, many things went wrong. Nell's, said the hostess to new arrivals, was the sort of place where people could drop in after a show and hear themselves talk. Keith observed that he hoped lots of octogenarians would come. 'Like, eighty-four-year-old ladies, in leather shorts', suggested little Nell. But the music was earsplitting. 'I thought you're supposed to be able to talk here,' bellowed a guest. 'What?' shrieked her companion.

Surveillance controllers, otherwise known as bouncers, hovered moodily in the shadow of 1930s' cut-glass lamps and chunky mirrors. Rupert Everett and Bianca Jagger and Andy Warhol ebbed and flowed. Drinks were poured by exquisite barmen chosen for their looks. 'Is not interesting,' said an Italian. 'Is very cheap.' Others were more enthusiastic. 'Man, this is a zoo,' remarked a male model. 'But stop by tomorrow night when this is all over with.'

He was right. Next evening, when the celebrities and the inquisitive riff-raff were no longer there, Nell's was functioning as its creators intended. As early as 10.00 p.m. opening time people were wandering in to sprawl on the ubiquitous sofas and to talk by the quiet light of candles. This is rare, if not unique, in a city where every club is jumping

with the pitiless thud of amplified funk. Nell feels that even New Yorkers are reacting against the aggression and incivility that pervade their town.

Already she has extended regal greetings to Madonna and Calvin Klein, though her biggest thrill was when Régine, monarch of the European night clubs, paid her $5 subscription fee just like anyone else. Despite the apparent homeliness of the place, however, care is taken to keep out people who aren't wanted. Chief among these are suburbanites who drive in to New York by the thousands each weekend and spread an unfashionable contagion which has been known to destroy other clubs. The telephone,

never still, often resounds with their enquiries. If they have a Brooklyn accent and the scream of babies is heard in the background they are given the wrong address.

'We try to be fair though,' says Nell. 'It's just that I want the place to be full of interesting and stylish people who I want to talk to. As there are some real burnt-out alley cats on the New York club circuit, I'm also keen to keep them out. But we insist the doormen are extra polite to the people they have to turn away.'

She hopes the club will supply the perfect background for dressing up and will encourage girls to wear 'that backless, strapless little black dress'. From ten at night until four in the morning she plays her part amid scruffy oil paintings and walls 'distressed' to give an illusion of Pompeian antiquity.

Red-haired, saucy, Little Nell presides with antipodean gusto in a setting that resembles the interior of a smart Portobello Road junk shop.

disco burn-out?

Disco burn-out is the usual fate of ventures into the war-zone of New York nightclubs. They are said to open and close within as short a period as six months.

Nell is unconcerned. However much of a celebrity she may be, she looks on what she is doing as just another role. Each night she dresses for the part, and each night the adrenalin bubbles. This time, though, she is her own scriptwriter and provides her own lines. As an actress she has known difficult times and periods when there was no money coming in. Now she hopes to make a lot of it.

◄ LITTLE NELL JUBILANT AS COLUMBIA

RAYNER BOURTON

ROCKY
no poof

Rocky came to life for the first time on any stage in the person of Rayner Bourton. Tall, virile, ruggedly handsome, Bourton gave a lyrical poignance to the role which made it a peculiarly moving creation. Rocky, he insists, is no poof. His exquisite wife, an Australian actress, would agree.

Born in Birmingham, vintage 1950, he got experience in provincial repertory theatres and touring. His first appearance on the professional stage was in *Hamlet* with Richard Chamberlain. He followed this at the Chichester Festival Theatre in *Caesar and Cleopatra* which starred Sir John Gielgud and Dame Edith Evans. Then he joined the National Theatre Company in their production of Peter Shaffer's *Equus*. This brought him up to 1973, year of *The Rocky Horror Show*.

Initially he planned to audition for the role of Dr Frank'n'Furter. Almost immediately Jim Sharman decided that his hair was too short and cast him, instead, as Rocky. It is one of the most difficult parts in the show, for Rocky needs to be a fully accomplished actor, singer, dancer and acrobat. He must also, in Rayner's interpretation, be able to suggest pathos and tenderness in his relationship with Frank.

Like everyone else Rayner has pleasant memories of the rehearsals. The cast, all on a flat wage of £18 a week, had no star nonsense about them. There were nine of them plus four players in the band, two designers of costume and scenery, a director, and lighting people. 'We all went in thinking, OK, here we are, we do three weeks of this unusual gig . . . just the three-week run of the play: that's all we went in for. When we got together, there was so much love between all the people in the play, more than in any show I've ever been with. Just incredible.'

The skeleton began to take on flesh. Some of the best ideas came from inspired improvisation. Since another play was being performed down below at conventional theatre times in the Royal Court, *The Rocky Horror Show* could not begin until late at night because of the noise it made. The usherettes, fearful of missing their last train home, refused to work overtime. It was Jim Sharman's brainwave to suggest that members of the cast wearing ghoulish masks should take over their job and, turning necessity into virtue, present one of the show's most original features.

The original three-week run was extended to four, then five, then twelve. The critics' reviews were unusually warm. What is more, when *Rocky* transferred to the King's Road cinema all the critics of the leading nationals and weeklies came back to see it again. Other theatre people in the West End who, unable to see the show at the usual hours because they were working at the same time too, asked for special performances. These were put on for, among others, Lauren Bacall, Angela Lansbury and all the workers behind the scenes. 'Please,' they said, 'we loved it so much, would you do another show the following week?' So the cast did, revelling in the best kind of compliment from their peers.

Julie Covington was the first Janet Weiss, although she played the part for only a short time and was succeeded by Belinda Sinclair, a veteran from *Hair*. One of her numbers with Rayner as Rocky involved a very intricate dance routine which, even at the best of times, was difficult to perform within the confines of the tiny stage. Once, despatched by Rocky with a vigorous spin, she whirled across and smashed into a heavy pillar. Bemused and half-unconscious, she nevertheless went on singing beautifully and completed the routine. Next day, unvanquished, she turned up as usual, regardless of a face badly swollen and hideously bruised.

Rocky goes to Tokyo

Rayner left the show after a while, although he sometimes returned as a guest to play Rocky, as on the third anniversary of its opening and on other signal occasions. He acted for a time, as had Tim Curry, with the Glasgow Citizens' Theatre, and then widened his experience on trips to Europe, Russia and the Far East. Back in England he compiled the revue *Off the Peg* which played for two seasons in Oxford and London. Another production, *Beggar My Neighbour*, was written entirely by him.

At the same time he developed his career as a rock singer. His Bowie-like voice was heard in singles like 'So long, Rudi', on the Columbia label, and in several albums. He put together a musical called *Let the Good Stones Roll* based on the music and reported sayings of the Rolling Stones which did well in the West End at the Ambassador's Theatre. On television he played in thrillers and, with Michael York and Penelope Keith, in *Much Ado About Nothing*. His versatility makes him as much at ease in rock as he is in Shakespeare.

The Rocky Horror Show, by now a multi-million-dollar thing, was travelling the world. In 1975 Rayner went with it to Japan as director and as actor in his original part of Rocky. The show was so successful that another visit followed in 1976. One of his cherished possessions is the programme which contains a side-by-side translation of the script from English into the elegant brush-strokes of Japanese ideographs.

On the first trip to Japan the original director Jim Sharman looked in for a week. 'As much as I enjoyed what you do,' he said, 'there is one mistake you're making: you're creating a parody of a parody.' On reflection Rayner agreed. 'The show must be played "for real" and straight, absolutely. That's the way it comes across best.'

In Japan, however, since they were playing in English the language barrier made it necessary to overdo the business slightly and to 'telegraph' the meaning. With that proviso Sharman's remark was wholly apt. 'It's not so much what you say,' adds Rayner, 'it's *how* you say it. Then it works as well as in other places where they understand our language.'

Exotic though *The Rocky Horror Show* may have seemed at first, the Japanese were able to detect unexpected similarities with their national Kabuki drama. In this highly stylized traditional form of theatre the women's roles are invariably acted by men. Another feature is the *hana-michi*, or 'flower way', a gangway running down one side of the theatre to the stage at a level with the heads of the audience. Along this the characters make their exits and their entrances, sometimes retiring into it to deliver asides and soliloquies. English audiences were startled by the novelty of actors making an entrance from the body of the theatre on ramps or stairs and not, according to convention, from stage left or right or centre. For the Japanese the process was familiar and something with which they could identify. *The Rocky Horror Show* was, to them, in several respects by no means so unusual as it had seemed to London spectators.

RAYNER BOURTON (ROCKY) BEING ADMIRED BY TIM CURRY (FRANK) ▶

レイナーボートン

ロッキーホラーショー

Apart from its resemblance to Kabuki *The Rocky Horror Show* took Tokyo by surprise. Newspapers reviewed it at length and it was frequently mentioned on radio and television. Media coverage, in short, was intense. And yet, despite all the apparent interest, houses were by no means full and audiences were puzzlingly small.

When, however, the company moved on to Osaka they started attracting capacity numbers, and in the weeks that followed, as they moved from Fukuoka to Oita, from Takamatsu to Kyoto, from Hakodate to Akita and Sendai, the box-office sold out. The same thing happened on their return for a season in Tokyo where, at their first visit, audiences had been so small.

The British Ambassador provided a solution to the enigma. Deeply schooled in the customs of the country, long aware that things are seldom what they seem in a society whose workings are controlled by innumerable subtleties and elaborate transactions behind the scenes, he explained that the promoter of *The Rocky Horror Show* had neglected to take into account the Yakuza, the equivalent of the Japanese Mafia. The result was empty seats in Tokyo. By the time the company reached Osaka the promoter had made amends to the Yakuza. From then on, and at the return to Tokyo, business flourished.

Acting Rocky each night and exploring Tokyo by day, Rayner found 'Ultra City', as it is known, an agreeable place. The rest of the cast thought so too. The Japanese had a great respect for each other, he decided, and he thought the West could learn from such an attitude. Tipping in restaurants and elsewhere did not exist, there was always somewhere to eat and drink regardless of what time of day or night it might be, and taxis were perpetually available. The reverse of the medal was the way artists were treated. In Japan they were owned by impresarios. They were not asked to do something or go somewhere, they were ordered. They had no protection and no one to safeguard their interests. Things were different in Britain. Yet the interchange suggested lessons for both countries.

So the tour went on through what guide-books like to call 'the islands of the electric sun'. At Yomiuriland the cast took part in a World Rock Concert surrounded by teeming crowds of chanting, dancing, screaming Japanese youth. One of the singers was pulled off the stage by a throng of excited fans while Rayner and the others fought nobly to get him back. The crowd won.

With the aid of their programme translations the Japanese soon learned to appreciate *The Rocky Horror show*, acutely Anglo-Saxon though it remained. Like Europeans, Americans, Scandinavians, Brazilians and Mexicans they adored Frank, admired Riff-Raff and loved Rocky. Crowds gathered nightly outside the theatre. Among them were many giggling Madame Butterflies. When Rayner appeared they rushed forward and some of them, laughing behind raised palms, blushing decorously, asked to take his chest measurements with a tape they had brought along. At last the bolder ones dared a quick hug, that having been, of course, the ultimate aim of the exercise. Upon which, bowing low and smiling '*domo arigato*', they melted away. It can be no coincidence that, amid the riot of Japanese lettering on the record album sleeve, there is one brief word in English which leaps out at you: it is SEX. What the context is only a Japanese scholar would know.

The

TIM CURRY (DR FRANK) HYMNS HIS CREATION (RAYNER BOURTON) W

Japanese mafia レイナーボート

.UMBIA (LITTLE NELL) LOOKS ON ADMIRINGLY

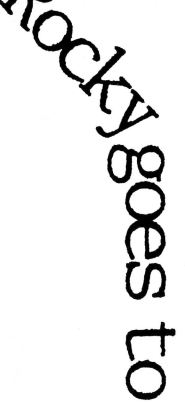

Rocky goes to

Six years after it opened at The Theatre Upstairs *The Rocky Horror Show* went to New Zealand. It had already been running three years in Australia and New Zealanders felt the time was overdue for tribute to an author who, if not born in their country, had at least spent most of his youth among them. Many of the cast were New Zealanders and they were supported, the producer stated proudly, by 'the backstage skills of many skilful Kiwis'. An indication of the showbusiness complexities involved is given by the legend which had to appear on all the promotion material: 'Stewart MacPherson's on behalf of Bees Knees Productions Limited by arrangement with Stetson Productions Harry M.Miller and by special arrangement with Michael White Limited proudly presents . . .'

Rayner Bourton went along, yet again, to direct and play his original part as Rocky. The show was the first entirely professional touring company of its kind to be organized in New Zealand. Special sets, props and costumes were re-created during three months of preparation. Technical equipment which was unavailable in New Zealand and could not be manufactured there had to be imported from Australia whence came the projector and a screen made of open shark's tooth gauze. The company of nearly thirty people travelled with sets carried in the biggest articulated truck New Zealand had ever seen.

Not to be out-glittered by Rayner's gold-encrusted Rocky, he stamped, pouted, posed and camped with a joyousness that delighted New Zealand audiences. Whether or not, as the promoters claimed, Richard O'Brien had him in mind as a part-inspiration when he wrote the show, he certainly made Frank, in the words of the song, a wild and an untamed thing. This came over with a particularly acid tang when he spat at the fearful Janet:

> Planet! Schmanet! Janet!
> I'll tell you once
> Won't tell you twice
> You'd better wise up, Janet Weiss.
> Y'apple pie
> Don't taste too nice
> You'd better wise up, Janet Weiss . . .
> . . . You'd better wise up — Janet Weiss
> You'd better wise up
> Build your thighs up
> You'd better wise up . . .

For eight weeks the giant articulated truck rumbled up and down New Zealand spreading the gospel 'Don't dream it, be it' around North and South Islands. Gary glittered, Rocky rolled, and the people of Hamilton, the town where Richard O'Brien misspent his early years, may well have exulted in the thought that their local boy had made good. On the other hand, they may not.

Dr Frank'n'Furter on the New Zealand tour was Gary Glitter, alias Paul Gadd of Oxfordshire, born 1944. As Paul Raven he had, since the age of fourteen, sparkled intermittently on the pop music scene. In 1972 he became Glitter by name and by image when he at last broke into the charts with 'Rock and Roll Part 2'. This was followed by numerous successes until in 1973, 'I Love You Love Me Love' earned him Britain's first platinum disc and an Ivor Novello award as the year's bestseller. But bad times were just around the corner. By 1975, just after he released 'Love Like You and Me', he had to leave England and spend some time in France as a tax exile. The company that was to present *The Rocky Horror Show* organized a New Zealand tour for him and his Glitter Band. It was logical that, when engaging the cast, they should have chosen him as Dr Frank'n'Furter.

GARY GLITTER ▶

the colour

Magenta is a small town in Italy. Here, more than a hundred years before *The Rocky Horror Show*, the French army defeated troops of the Austrian Empire in a battle which led eventually to Italian independence. A Paris boulevard was named in honour of the victory and so, too, was a new type of aniline dye, vividly crimson in colour, which was discovered soon afterwards. All this has nothing to do with the character called Magenta in *Rocky*, except, perhaps, that Richard O'Brien gave her the name because it sounded rather pretty.

The role of Magenta at The Theatre Upstairs was taken by Patricia Quinn. She also doubled as the Usherette who opens and closes the show with 'Science Fiction Double Feature'. In the film she repeated the part, and hers are the 'lewd and lascivious lips' which introduce the action. She is, irrevocably, Irish, and comes from Belfast where she was born on 28 May 1944. Soon after leaving school she went on stage in her native city and then, like Tim Curry and Rayner Bourton, got valuable training at the Glasgow Citizens' Theatre. She came to London and acted in *AC/DC*, one of the Royal Court's award-winning plays, and in *Stripwell*. After *The Rocky Horror Show*, in which she was succeeded during the long run by half a dozen other actresses, she played in *Murder, The Threepenny Opera* and various West End plays. On television she appeared, by way of a change, as Christabel Pankhurst, the redoubtable Suffragette. She remembers finishing a *Rocky Horror Show* performance late one Saturday night and taking the train for Halifax where, as Miss Pankhurst, she was to give a rip-roaring political speech. Since she was still covered from head to foot in glitter from *Rocky* the television wardrobe mistress had to camouflage it with a voluminous period dress.

She has made films like *Up the Chastity Belt, Rent-a-Dick* and *The Garnett Saga* featuring the immortal Alf. In *I, Claudius* she oozed sensuality as the sister of the decadent Roman tyrant. On American television she played opposite George C. Scott in *Beauty and The Beast*. Richard O'Brien's *Disaster* gave her a powerful role as the ambitious Martha Fortune. One of her most flamboyant appearances was as Sarah Bernhardt in *Sarah B. Divine,* where her red hair and sulky lips helped to recreate the aura of that unforgettable *monstre sacré*. From this to the part of Mrs John Cleese in *Monty Python's The Meaning of Life* might seem the shortest of steps.

'Yeah — you're lucky — I'm lucky — he's lucky — we're all lucky!' screams Magenta with an eldritch shriek when Janet congratulates Frank on having servants to look after him. She has no big numbers to sing but she is always hovering in the background, a domestic of unusually menacing nature. While Janet goes into 'Touch-a touch-a touch me' she and Columbia provide a mocking commentary as they sip ironically from their champagne glasses. Magenta is subtler than Columbia, the all-too-obvious groupie, and even speaks with a Shakespearian resonance on occasion, as witness her remark after Frank has put the artistes of the floor show into a molecular state: 'When do we return to Transylvania? — I grow weary of this world.'

As the action develops her presence becomes yet more sinister. 'Magenta,' Frank says to her, 'I am indeed grateful to both you and your brother Riff-Raff — you have both served me well. Loyalty such as yours must be rewarded, and you will discover that when the mood takes me, I can be quite generous.' He strokes her and puts his arm round her. She throws off his arm and snaps: 'I ask for nothing, Master.' He replies sweetly: 'And you shall receive it in abundance . . .'

Magenta

● ● ●

She exchanges the Transylvanian salute with Riff-Raff, arms held high-palms brought together, and goes out with him on what can only be a shady errand. Later, as Frank makes his last appeal in 'Going Home'

Cards for sorrow, cards for pain
I've seen blue skies
Through the tears in my eyes
And I realize – I'm going home

she yawns with boredom and comments, 'How sentimental'. The tables are turned, Frank is now the victim, and, dissolving with Riff-Raff into evil chuckles, Magenta activates the transit crystal while sardonically enquiring: 'I wonder if I remembered to cancel the milk?' A flash is seen, a bang is heard, and both characters vanish leaving behind a suspicion that her affection for him is rather more than sisterly, and his for her somewhat more than brotherly.

PAT QUINN (MAGENTA) AND
RICHARD O'BRIEN (RIFF-RAFF)

The entire house is beamed back to the planet of Transexual in the galaxy of Transylvania, where, doubtless, the ambiguous relationship still flourishes. The Usherette, strangely like Magenta despite her uniform and ice-cream tray, reappears and sings:

Darkness has conquered Brad and
Janet
The servants gone to a distant planet
Oh – at the late night double feature
Picture show – I want to go – ohh –
To the late night double feature picture
show.

The suggestive eyes and smouldering sexuality of Magenta are only one aspect of Pat Quinn. Off-stage, one is a little disappointed to find, she lives a life of exemplary virtue with her husband, the actor and director Don Hawkins, and a son whose name is . . . Quinn.

the colour Gray

Among the most distinguished of the Narrators to succeed Jonathan Adams is Charles Gray, who played the part in the film version. He comes from Bournemouth and brings with him something of the stateliness associated with that town. His background comprises the Stratford Royal Shakespeare Company, the Old Vic, and character roles as ambassadors, generals, noblemen and judges. Yet under the bland exterior there is an impish devil which bursts out from time to time in parts like that of Malvolio, the cracked fantastical steward in *Twelfth Night*, or the oily pimping Pandarus in *Troilus and Cressida*. As the Narrator observes: 'There are those who say that life is an illusion — and reality, as we know it, is merely a figment of our imaginations.'

On stage he has also played Sheridan Whiteside in *The Man Who Came to Dinner* based on the irrepressible American journalist Alexander Woollcott. His Broadway appearances include a Jean Anouilh play which won him an award as best supporting performer of the year and a co-starring role with Alfred Drake. He is, not unexpectedly, very much at home in the sophisticated atmosphere of Oscar Wilde's *Lady Windermere's Fan*, the witty dialogue of Shaw's *The Millionairess*, and the worldly cynicism of Maugham's *The Moon and Sixpence*. But the imp keeps bubbling up, nowhere more unexpectedly than when he played the dapper villain Blofeld in *Diamonds Are Forever* and, during his battle to outwit James Bond, got himself up in drag. He made an unforgettable matron complete with ghastly wig and jutting bosom.

Although his stage career has been a distinguished one, he prefers to work in films and television. He has been a haughty knight in *Upstairs Downstairs*, a commanding police officer in *Softly Softly*, an aristocratic father of the bride in *Charles and Diana — A Royal Love Story*, and a guest star in *Bergerac*. When his agent put to him the role of Narrator in *The Rocky Horror Show* he paused for a moment. Then the imp came to the surface and he replied innocently: 'Why not?'

It was possible, his agent went on, that a record might later be issued of the show. Prudence dictated that his contract should include provision for a royalty. Now the Narrator, you may remember, neither sings nor dances except for a handful of interventions in 'The Time Warp' and 'Eddie's Teddy'. During the first he advises, 'It's just a jump to the left,' and then, demonstrating the step on top of his desk, 'With your hands on your hips'. Afterwards, as Dr Scott laments the virtues of his dear departed nephew Eddie

From the day he was born, he was trouble
He was the thorn in his mother's side.
She tried in vain

the Narrator adds his comment with a deliciously uncharacteristic neglect of grammar: 'But he never caused her nothing but shame.' The record which was eventually released has sold many, many copies. For his brief interjections Charles Gray receives, every six months, a pleasing sum in royalties.

The Narrator, as Charles presents him, is as much a bravura performance as Dr Frank-

'n'Furter's. A hint of menace, a touch of outrage, a suggestion, even, that the audience is almost to blame for the horrors enacted in the story, make him a figure both amused and authoritative. He moralizes with a flowery earnestness that only serves to underline the comedy: 'If one is suffering the pangs of remorse for a sexual indiscretion — it would seem logical that the transgressor would be sympathetic towards a loved one caught committing a similar misdemeanour. But emotion is an irrational and powerful master — and from what Janet witnesses on the monitor — there seemed little doubt that she was indeed its slave.'

In the aftermath, when Brad and Janet have both suffered at the villainous hands of Dr Frank, the Narrator observes: 'And, just a few hours after announcing their engagement, Brad and Janet had both tasted forbidden fruit. This in itself was proof that their host was a man of little morals and some persuasion. What further indignities were they to be subjected to . . . ? And what of the sonic transducer and the floorshow that had been spoken of? What indeed? From what had gone before it was clear that this was to be no picnic.' The relish of the words, the sudden descent from orotund diction to the unexpected colloquialism at the end, are a trick worthy of Dickens at his most comic.

The scenes involving the Narrator, who does not move outside his book-lined study, were shot in two days. Charles Gray never met any other member of the cast and has never seen the film.

A few years later he appeared in Richard O'Brien's film *Shock Treatment*. Although sometimes described as a sequel to the Rocky show, it differs from it quite considerably. There were familiar faces in the cast — Richard O'Brien and Pat Quinn as brother and sister again, Little Nell as Nurse Ansalong, and Jeremy Newson who in the previous film had been Ralph Hapschatt — but the setting and action were entirely different. The scene is Denton television studios and a quiz game, 'Marriage Maze', presided over by a raving host, the blind Bert Schnick (Barry Humphries). Among the competing couples are Brad and Janet, of whom the former ends up in a lunatic asylum run by the demented Cosmo McKinley (Richard O'Brien). In *Shock Treatment* the equivalent of 'The Time Warp' is a lively number called 'Look What They Did to my ID'. Through it all, his aplomb undisturbed by the punkish revels that explode around him, moves Charles Gray as Judge Oliver Wright accompanied by an effervescent Ruby Wax. At the finale, however, his reserve breaks down and he throws himself into an energetic song and

dance number which makes one fear for his safety — indeed, at one point he trips over a chair but recovers himself so adroitly that the director kept the shot as it stood. This alone makes *Shock Treatment,* or *Shocky* as it is known to devotees, worth seeing, although it includes many other pleasures: brilliant one-liners of vintage O'Brien, foot-tapping tunes, and Barry Humphries at his campest as the Viennese shrink.

CHARLES GRAY

In Charles Gray's subsequent career events have sometimes recalled *The Rocky Horror Show*. He recently appeared with Coral Browne, Vincent Price's wife, in a National Theatre production of *Oedipus Rex*. At one point the chorus bore in a huge phallic symbol. Miss Browne turned to Charles and, in a voice that reverberated well into the stalls, observed: 'Nobody we know, dear . . . unfortunately.'

Rocky ancient and modern

*T*he *Rocky Horror Show* is at once very new and very old, very contemporary and very traditional. The comedies of Aristophanes, 400 years before the birth of Christ, present just such a loosely concocted mixture of obscenity and buffoonery, of topicality and invective, as does *Rocky*. The women's roles, moreover, were played by men, while the leading comic actors wore flesh-coloured tights and a huge leather phallus, often painted red. In the old Greek legends bisexuality was not unknown and is typified by the soothsayer Tiresias. He, according to Ovid, once beheld two snakes copulating and hit them, no one knows why, with his staff, for which he was turned into a woman. Seven years later he witnessed the snakes at it again, belaboured them with his staff once more and was turned back into a man. From then on he was regarded as an authority on sex, having known it, so to speak, in both capacities. When the god Zeus and the goddess Hera argued the topic of whether a man or a woman derives more pleasure from sex, he, given his experience, was called in to adjudicate. His decision was that women got nine times more enjoyment from it than did men. The prim Hera was so outraged that she struck him blind. Zeus, more tolerant, bestowed upon him the gifts of long life and prophecy.

If Dr Frank'n'Furter peeps coyly out of the mists of Greek antiquity, Riff-Raff may also be glimpsed in the ancient Roman comedies. Among the stock characters of rustic farces there was always a hunchbacked slave who attended his master and served him with dubious loyalty, often intriguing behind his back. For a time these early prototypes vanished from sight while the Christian church established itself. In the Middle Ages worshippers had begun to act out scenes from the liturgy inside churches. When the performances grew too elaborate and crowded they moved outside into the open air and the theatre was re-born. A central comic figure of the mediaeval plays was Satan himself. His retinue consisted of devils who, at the Last Judgement, shovelled, lost souls into hell with gleeful relish. He was, like Dr Frank'n'Furter, a villain steeped in black arts whom the audience loved to hate.

There was spectacle besides. The mouth of Hell gaped open and belched out clouds of smoke like the dry ice in the current touring production of *Rocky*. The bloodied limbs and severed heads which mediaeval technicians faked up for realism are paralleled by the plastic bag containing Eddie's mangled remains which Frank contemptuously bids Magenta put down the waste disposal. The earthquakes, floods and fires contrived by sixteenth-century stage-hands aroused as much admiration as do lasers today.

Brad and Janet emerge from the Italian *commedia dell'arte* in the sixteenth and seventeenth centuries. They are the young lovers who, not very interesting in themselves, give an excuse for the action of the plot. Handsome and attractive though they may be, they are merely characters around whom events take place.

The influence of the *commedia dell'arte* travelled via several of the characters — Arlecchino, Colombina and Pantalone — to England and made up the Harlequinade which became nineteenth-century pantomime and music-hall. Harlequin was supposed to have been born from an egg, like Rocky in the current production. He had a magic sword which, in the manner of Dr

Frank'n'Furter's sonic transducer, could immobilize enemies and put them out of action.

By the time the traditional pantomime had begun to flourish all the elements of *The Rocky Horror Show* were in place. Cross-dressing was the business of the Principal Boy, always a girl with beautiful legs, and the comic Dame was usually a low comedian who specialized in buffoonery. Pantomime writers like to emphasize that men have been dressing up as women for fun ever since the Bacchanalian revels of the Roman age. They also point out that in the classic drama of China and Japan the tradition still exists.

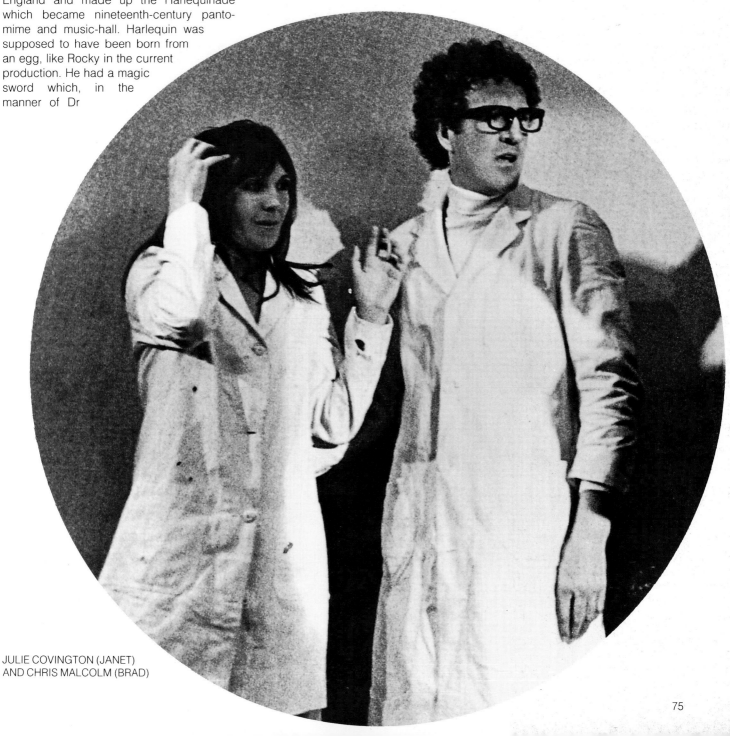

JULIE COVINGTON (JANET)
AND CHRIS MALCOLM (BRAD)

Often the villain was a Demon King, horned, tailed, clad in red robes and shooting up amid smoke and flames through a trap door. He was the predecessor of Dr Frank, an apparition which made the audience shiver with delight and roar abuse. The hunchbacked slave of Greek comedy became the page Buttons or man Friday in *Robinson Crusoe*, who is reincarnated as Riff-Raff. The terrifying adventures of Brad and Janet had long since been foreshadowed by the plot of *Babes in the Wood*. The transformation scene which every pantomime had as its grand finale, an affair of glittering tinsel and gorgeous colours, is today supplied by lasers that fill the theatre with shifting walls of unearthly light.

So Frank is the Demon King, the Principal Boy, the Ogre, the Ugly Sister and the Dame all in one. Riff-Raff is Buttons, Clown, Harlequin and Dick Whittington's Cat. They speak in couplets which are drolly flat-footed. An exchange like this, where the Fairy Queen accepts a calf for the magic beans in *Jack and the Beanstalk*:

Fairy Queen: *Well, give the calf.*
Jack: *I do!*
Fairy Queen: *The beans are thine.*
Jack: *Though this transaction bears a strange character*
I look upon you as my beanyfactor'

is equalled in scansion and rhyme by the salutation to Frank:

You're a hot dog
But you'd better not try to hurt her
Frank Furter.

Likewise the audience participation in *Rocky* is nothing new and has been a feature of pantomimes for over a century. 'Oh yes I am!' roars the Demon King, or the genie in *Aladdin*, or the Wicked Fairy. 'Oh no you're not!' screams the audience, repeating a dialogue consecrated by the ages. To help them in the community singing that follows the words of the song are projected on a screen or shown on boards while Buttons indicates the lines with a pointer. This is what Riff-Raff does in the course of Brad's song when the ghouls obligingly display the words of the chorus written out on large pieces of card. Only in one respect does pantomime go further: at certain points members of the audience, usually children, are invited up on to the stage and take part in the action. This is something the management of *Rocky* take every precaution to avoid, and for good reason.

RAYNER BOURTON (ROCKY) IS UNVEILED BY RICHARD O'BRIEN (RIFF-RAFF) AND TIM CURRY (FF

Damocles ignotus

The predominantly youthful audiences at *The Rocky Horror Show* are not put off by references to old films and cult figures which existed years before they were born. The film has many touches that can be appreciated only by veteran movie addicts. Frank's corpse bobs around in a swimming pool that recalls the scene of William Holden's body floating in a classic shot from *Sunset Boulevard*. Rocky clambers up the RKO tower as King Kong scrambled up the Empire State Building. Dr Scott is a reminiscence of Dr Strangelove. The spectacle of the characters fraternizing in a slow-motion underwater ballet is a satirical footnote to many an Esther Williams swimming show. Paintings are wittily used. While Brad serenades Janet, Riff-Raff and Magenta pose by the church door looking as if they have just stepped out of that famous picture 'American Gothic', he in granny glasses and collarless shirt and holding a pitchfork, she with hair severely scraped back and wearing a pinafore. A reproduction of the picture is to be seen next to an up-ended coffin as Riff-Raff launches on the 'Time Warp' song. Then, during 'Eddie's Teddy', at a reference to the mother who despaired of his low taste for rock'n'roll porn and shooting up junk, there is a quick flash of the celebrated painting 'Whistler's Mother'. But is it the actual canvas? Few people realize that the features which peep out benevolently from under the mob cap are those of Meatloaf.

In the interests of research an audience of undergraduates aged eighteen and nineteen was polled on the names and titles mentioned in *The Rocky Horror Show*. They all knew about Flash Gordon and King Kong and could say who the characters were. Frankenstein and Buddy Holly were generally recognized, though the latter, while correctly described as wearing glasses, was in one case identified as a male stripper. *The Day Of The Triffids* and *Tarantula* scored reasonably high marks for recognition as did Charles Atlas with eighty per cent. Fay Wray and Transylvania came next, closely followed by RKO Radio, UFOs and Steve Reeves. From this point onwards familiarity declined. Only fifty per cent knew about Jeanette Scott and *Forbidden Planet*. Even fewer had come across *When Worlds Collide* and Leo G.

Carrol. Less than twenty per cent could identify Dana Andrews, classified in one response as an actress, or Lilly St Cyr. No one knew about George Pal, the Hungarian puppeteer who became one of the cleverest designers of science fiction films. Less excusably, the Sword of Damocles, which is the motif of Rocky's birthday song —

> *The Sword of Damocles is hanging*
> *over my head*
> *And I've got the feeling someone's*
> *Going to be cutting the thread*
> *Oh woe is me — my life is a misery*
> *Oh can't you see that I'm at the start*
> *Of a pretty big downer*
> *I woke up this morning with a start*
> *when*
> *I fell out of bed . . .*

was unknown to all. Still, the ghost of Claude Raines must be satisfied: fifty per cent described him as 'a great actor'.

Ignorance of cult references in *The Rocky Horror Show* is, therefore, no bar to enjoyment. Other factors must be looked at. Audience involvement is positively encouraged by the Narrator from the very beginning. 'I would like — if I may — to take you on a strange journey,' he says, addressing himself directly to his listeners. From time to time in his commentary he intervenes with rhetorical questions which, as all politicians know, arouse an irresistible tendency to answer back. His air of mock authority and simulated horror invite conspiratorial amusement. Before long the audience is laughing both at him and with him. Collusion is soon established between stage and auditorium.

The spectators have always played a vital part in the theatre. Without them there can be no play. In their absence the actors and actresses have nothing to stimulate their art, nothing to guide their shaping of effects. As the history of pantomime demonstrates, the audience can itself take on a more positive and vocal role. In modern times this has been emphasized by television shows where members of the audience can be the main performers. *The Price is Right* and phone-in programmes on radio have proved Andy Warhol's dictum that everyone has the chance of being famous for a minute or two in this electronic age.

Le plus terrifiant des vampires !

DRACULA

avec

BELA LUGOSI · DAVID MANNERS
HELEN CHANDLER · DWIGHT FRYE

Une Production TOD BROWNING
Produit par CARL LAEMMLE Jr.
Réalisé par TOD BROWNING

Distribué par **UNIVERSAL**

Universal International

DRACULA
in baked beans

LOOK-ALIKES – PART OF THE 'TRAVELLING AUDIENCE' THAT ACCOMPANIES THE CURRENT *ROCKY* TOUR

Where *The Rocky Horror Show* takes participation a step further is in the custom audiences have acquired of dressing up like the cast themselves. At Nottingham Theatre Royal a local critic was taken aback at seeing in the foyer a group of what looked like trainee doctors adjusting their white coats. Down the stairs minced a husky fellow in red satin basque and fishnet stockings. Around the doors into the auditorium clustered a girl wearing a black leotard with an L-plate on her back, a surgeon in a green operating gown and wellington boots, a visitor from outer space, men who appeared to have left their trousers at home, and an assortment of people drained of blood, lank of hair, got up as schoolgirls, domestics, tarts and vampires.

In Birmingham visits by the touring company of *The Rocky Horror Show* are occasions of riotous assembly. On one such the bar staff at the Hippodrome all dressed up as well in honour of the show. The stalls barman disguised himself as Dracula. When, at half-time, the audience roared into the bar, they peppered him with baked beans and tomato ketchup. At the height of the excitement an SOS came that a woman was locked in the lavatory. The gallant barman, arrayed in his Dracula rig, squeezed through the packed women's lavatories and, dripping beans and ketchup on the floor, unscrewed the door. While he performed his mission of mercy a pair of Magentas showered him with relentless squirts from their water pistols.

A Guide Captain who brought a party of her girls to see *The Rocky Horror Show* at the Grand Theatre in Leeds became apprehensive as the audience seethed and whirled around her. After the curtain rose she nervously wondered if she had done right in exposing her tender charges to such an experience. By the end of the show, after the ritual deluge of rice, chocolate bars, water and chips, she was on her feet dancing and singing along with all the nuns, mini-skirted tramps and lads in suspender belts. The exaltation engendered by *Rocky* tends to be catching.

Although *The Rocky Horror Show* has an enthusiastic gay following, it attracts heterosexual fans in equal numbers. Among the weirdly caparisoned audience there are as many rugger hearties tricked out in suspenders as there are macho beefies in black stockings who have brought along girl friends robed like Magenta and Columbia. Why do they dress up? Because, like wearing earrings and torn blue jeans and cockatoo hair-cuts, it is a fashion to do so. Another explanation emphasizes that, for the inarticulate, dress is a way of expressing oneself. You may be dumb, you may totally lack eloquence, but what you wear can do the talking for you. Clothes can make contact on your behalf and can tell others things which

...DRACULA
in baked beans

you lack the ability to say. They are also a reaction to, a colourful shout of despair against, the dull daily routine which comprises the majority of lives. As for the exultant barracking and rowdyism which accompany performances of *The Rocky Horror Show*, they represent a safety valve that is shared by the exuberance of football team supporters.

When a critic asked Sam Goldwyn about the 'message' of his films, the veteran producer is said to have joked: 'If I got a message I always send it by Western Union.' In creating *The Rocky Horror Show* Richard O'Brien had no conscious message to deliver. As Paul Valéry observed, a poem is never finished, even when the poet has written the final line. The work of art is there, to be used by anyone else who cares as a piece of equipment is used, for any purpose and for any theory. The readers, the critics, the audiences take it up and put into it what they please.

The moral of *Rocky* is, of course, 'Don't dream it, be it', which is taken largely in its sexual connotation. 'I must admit,' says Richard O'Brien, 'that, were I writing it today, because of sexual disease, I'd be very careful about the sexual do-your-own-thing idea.' Looking back over the fifteen years of *Rocky*'s buoyant existence and studying the vast crowds it still draws today, he adds: 'Why has it lasted so long? Well, from day one it has attracted people who aren't traditional theatre-goers. And that's got to be good. It has three major elements. Sex, rock'n'roll and Gothic horror — not a bad threesome — and each has its own following. Plus it unlocks, reexamines old myths. And it was prophetic of punk. Of Boy George. Of Prince — there is an element of his narcissism in Frank.'

In America professional students of what they call 'sexual trauma' have decreed that *The Rocky Horror Show* provides an outlet which fans cannot obtain anywhere else. However confused you may be, runs the theory, you can learn from *Rocky* the assurance that there is nothing wrong in cross-dressing, in donning a corset and suspender belt. For an hour or two you can live in a world that never was, a world that banishes reality and wraps you in cloud-capped dreams.

While *The Rocky Horror Show* can be said to advocate, in its flip wisecracking way, the route to sexual liberation, it also argues for freedom on a wider scale. If, at times, it seems to be a plea for absolute hedonism, at others it oddly echoes the self-help philosophy of Samuel Smiles. As Richard O'Brien has earlier been quoted in this book, the moral is to get up and do things. If you dream of writing a novel, or climbing a mountain, or riding a winner, go out and write it, climb it, ride it. The paradox of *Rocky* is that while it exemplifies twentieth-century permissiveness, at the same time it encourages Victorian ideals of self-reliance.

MORE FANS OF THE SHOW

the one you found_ she is gone_ And that's all the ti

a - bout some one you thought you'd known

2 (Janet sings harmony)

So ba - by don't cry_

Alice and Rocky

In the nineteenth century the words of popular music were written according to strict rules of prosody and metre. W.S.Gilbert composed verse in which the grammar was immaculate and the rhymes clicked into place with unfailing precision:

> I am the very model of a modern major-
>   general,
> I've information vegetable, animal and
>   mineral;
> I know the kings of England, and I
>   quote the fights historical
> From Marathon to Waterloo, in order
>   categorical;
> I'm very well acquainted too with mat-
>   ters mathematical;
> I understand equations, both the sim-
>   ple and quadratical;
> About binomial theorem I'm teeming
>   with a lot o'news,
> With many cheerful facts about the
>   square of the hypotenuse.

In the music-hall, too, however slangy or idiomatic the refrain, the conventions of rhyme and metre were usually observed, as when Harry Champion sang:

> I'm 'enery the Eighth, I am!
> 'enery the Eighth I am, I am!
> I got married to the widow next door,
> She's been married seven times be-
>   fore.
> Ev'ryone was a 'enery —
> She wouldn't have a Willie or a Sam.
> I'm her eighth old man named 'enery,
> 'enery the Eighth I am, I am!
> 'enery the Eighth I am!'

With the arrival of rock music all this changed. Verse was succeeded by recitative in which lines of varying length hit occasionally on a rhyme by happy accident. In *The Rocky Horror Show* Brad sings a mixture of assonance and vague inner rhymes:

> Once in a while
> She don't want to call you
> Speaking on the telephone
> And once in your life
> She won't want to know you
> You look around
> The one you found she is gone.
> And that's all the time
> That it takes
> For a heart to turn to stone
> The sweeter the wine
> The harder to make the break
> You hear something
> About someone you thought you'd
>   known
> So, baby, don't cry
> Like there's no tomorrow
> After the night there's brand new day
> And there'll be no pain
> And no more sorrow.

The precise techniques of W. S. Gilbert and Cole Porter are replaced by lines that follow more closely the rhythms of everyday speech and, occasionally, an aleatory rhyme to remind us that this is a lyric.

With *The Rocky Horror Show*, says that bible of modern life *Men in Frocks*, 'here beginneth trash drag, here beginneth much of the look of punk. The world has never been the same since.' Before *Rocky*, however, there was Alice Cooper. Even today, when he teeters on the dread age of forty, Alice is still

(Brad solo) So wash your face

... Alice and Rocky

at it. On stage he lollops maniacally through a Gothic setting of cobwebbed junkery slashing his whip and transfixing baby dolls with a sword. 'Be my lover,' he coos to the python he fondles adoringly. 'Go to hell,' he screams as he crosses whips with a dyke in leather. 'I love the dead,' he croaks while the guillotine rattles. The stage fills with dismembered legs and heads and arms. More to the point, one of his most popular numbers is 'Teenage Frankenstein', which takes us on to Rocky.

The music of *The Rocky Horror Show*, call it trash punk or what you will, is memorable and insidious. It is characterized by figurations that circulate closely around a given note and rarely venture away from it beyond the interval of a third. In 'Science Fiction Double Feature' the melody, apart from the anacrusis, settles repeatedly on F and is reluctant to leave it except for a jump of a fifth on 'Then something went wrong' and a sudden leap of an octave with 'They got caught in a celluloid jam'. The device of repeating the note creates a hypnotic feeling, as if a bubble were growing until, abruptly, it bursts and dissolves the tension. This is the trick used by Ravel in *Boléro* and it never fails.

The same technique gives urgency to 'The Time Warp' with its ominous thudding introduction and sudden triumphant blaze into *tierces de Picardie* when everyone jubilates 'Let's do the Time Warp again!' Again, it adds a stabbing emphasis to Frank's powerful declaration 'I'm just a sweet transvestite from Transexual Transylvania' and the ghoulish trill on the last syllable. One of the most effective uses of repetition occurs in Riff-Raff's declaration to Frank:

Frank'n'Furter
It's all over
Your mission is a failure
Your life style's too extreme
I'm your new commander
You are now my prisoner.

The constantly sounded F against a background of identical block chords is nothing more nor less than recitative as employed by Gounod and his like in nineteenth-century grand opera.

Other elements colour the score and produce moments of unexpected charm. 'Over at the Frankenstein place' contains passages of close harmony, barbershop fashion, which blend sweetness and sincerity. Frank's 'I'm a wild and an untamed thing' has the unmistakeable ring of bouncy music-hall songs associated with Marie Lloyd and Harry Champion. By contrast, 'Don't dream it, be it', gently rises and falls to an accompaniment of flowing triplets and lulls the ear with genuine yearning. Even more nostalgic is the four-bar motif that introduces 'Superheroes'. As if ashamed of being caught in an open display of feeling, it then wanders off up and down the keyboard, only to sneak back and underline the Narrator's final words:

And crawling on the planet's face
Some insects called the human race
Lost in time
And lost in space
And meaning.

This untypically poignant mood is quickly swept away by a reprise of 'Science Fiction, Double Feature' and the other more clamant numbers. But the memory of it remains to haunt the mind, and its innocent tinkle is only one of the attractions in a score which stays as vivid and vital as it sounded over a decade ago when it was first heard.

why Stoke-on-Trent?

From the Midlands have come many of the finest things in English life: the plays of Shakespeare; Johnson and his Dictionary; china by Wedgwood, Spode and Minton; the novels of Arnold Bennett; *Cross-roads* . . . and the touring production of *The Rocky Horror Show*.

In 1841 Mr Elphinstone of Hanley, Stoke-on-Trent, bought a plot of land on a slope now known as Pall Mall. There he built a theatre narrow of façade and sturdy in the early Victorian tradition of architecture. He called it the Theatre Royal. His fellow citizens repaid him by attending assiduously and ensuring that it flourished for a century. However, by 1980 the place was 'dark' and only kept going as a Mecca bingo hall. But the charms of bingo were also fading and Mecca could see little future for the building.

Others were more optimistic, among them a local solicitor called Charles Deacon. As a child he had regularly been to annual Christmas pantomimes at the Theatre Royal which left him with enduring memories and a love of the stage. A charitable trust was set up to rescue and restore the theatre with Charles Deacon as its chairman. His fellow trustees included John E. Jones who does not resemble the tax inspector he once was. Behind his genial manner lies the keen financial expertise which qualified him to become secretary to the limited company that now runs the Theatre Royal where he is also general manager.

In the summer of 1982 the trustees entered the theatre to find it in a lamentable state. A harsh winter had burst pipes and ruined interiors. There was no effective central heating or plumbing. Timbers were rotting, brickwork was cracked and stairs were sagging. Decay and desolation hung in the air. After long discussions Mecca leased the property to the Trust and granted an option to buy the freehold for £200,000. The option had to be exercised by August 1984.

The trustees decided that they needed to raise £500,000. In addition to the sum required for the freehold they calculated that another £300,000 was essential to repair, redecorate, rewire and meet the cost of stage equipment. Why should they bother? Because, the Trust agreed, Stoke-on-Trent was the largest conurbation in Great Britain without a traditional touring theatre. Although television had helped to close many theatres during the 1960s, the recent arrival of video

recording meant that potential audiences were no longer committed to their sets in the evening and that theatres could benefit accordingly. The 'live' theatre, the Trust continued, was an essential training ground for actors and dramatists, and encouragement of it would promote new productions and interest in the arts. Moreover, volunteers who helped run the theatre would find valuable and creative occupations for their increasing leisure time.

These arguments, promoted with vigour and publicized with dedication, were successful. Under the patronage of the Earl of Litchfield the Trust was able, very shortly, to buy the freehold and launch extensive repairs. Throughout the whole appeal the balance between money and art was subtly preserved.

The Theatre Royal Hanley, as it is officially described, went 'live' again in 1983 with a Christmas production of *Aladdin*. It could now seat 1500 people and supply them with drinks in three licensed bars. Casts were accommodated in eleven dressing rooms and green room. There was space for over thirty musicians in the pit. The proscenium, glinting with new paint, fronted a stage more than seventy metres wide and ten metres deep. Since, however, the Theatre Royal was unsubsidised and received not a penny from the Arts Council or the municipality, one last difficult problem remained: what was to be put on that stage so lovingly restored, and how to fill that auditorium so beautifully decorated, in order to attract the revenue so desperately needed?

The answers were supplied with the arrival of Paul Barnard, a well-known figure on the provincial theatre circuit, and John Farrow, his colleague as executive producer. Since then the theatre has become extremely successful. Many productions originating in Hanley have gone on to tour theatres elsewhere. *Once a Catholic*, which starred Fenella Fielding, was among the earliest ones. More elaborate shows with full musical backing such as *They're Playing Our Song* and Ivor Novello's *Perchance to Dream*, the latter headed by Simon Ward, also went out on tour after popular seasons at the Theatre Royal. In less than a year attractions ranging from *The Wind in the Willows* to *Run for Your Wife*, by way of *Steaming* and *Educating Rita* to *Billy Liar* and *The Sound of Murder*, held the stage of the theatre. One of the most successful

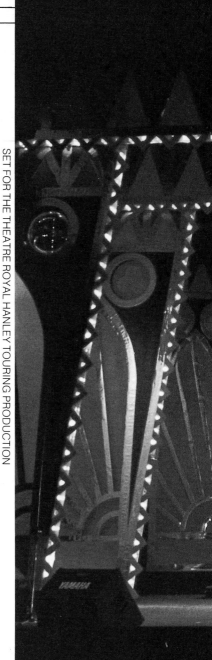

SET FOR THE THEATRE ROYAL HANLEY TOURING PRODUCTION

JOHN E JONES

JOHN FARROW

has been the revival of *Cabaret* featuring Wayne Sleep, which found a long-running niche in the West End. Another West End success from Hanley is *The Hobbit*. The traffic is now two-way. While acting as host to productions from London the Theatre Royal also sends its own to the capital.

Since the Theatre Royal needs anything up to fifty different attractions a year to draw audiences there is always a lively debate about what should be done next. In the summer of 1984 *The Rocky Horror Show* was mentioned. Four years earlier it had completed its phenomenal London run and had already been staged in Paris, Tokyo, New Zealand, Australia, Frankfurt, Oslo, Brazil and Los Angeles. The provincial touring rights were available. Was it not now the turn of Stoke-on-Trent?

The rights were taken up and auditions held. Vivyan Ellacott, artistic director of the Kenneth More Theatre in Ilford, Essex, was chosen to direct, and Paul Barnard produced, the show which John Farrow continues to supervise. The sets, consisting of Frank's castle seen from outside and an interior of his laboratory, were designed and painted by Ian Wilson. The choreography was the work of Lorraine Porter and Nigel Ellacott designed the costumes. Malcolm Sircom, musical director at the Theatre Royal, who is as brilliantly at ease with the lush romanticism of Ivor Novello as he is with the raw rock of Richard O'Brien, led from the keyboard an ensemble of drums, bass, guitar and saxophone.

bombs and bags

Few people, at this stage, realized what a large role the audience was going to claim for itself or how its reaction was to dominate the mood of performances. Everyone knew that in America the film attracted packed houses of look-alikes who threw things at the screen and ad-libbed dialogue as the action developed. So far, in England, the film version was the object of an intense but limited coterie. Even so, at the Times Centa Cinema off Baker Street it had run continuously for more than five years after which the management, although it still did good business, had taken it off except for occasional late-night presentations. They had grown tired of the damage constantly inflicted on the screen. The rice, strangely enough, did not do so much damage as the flour which took days to clean from the seats. Eggs had cost them a number of screens. Enough, they decided, was enough.

The Theatre Royal production of *The Rocky Horror Show* made its debut in Hanley on 7 June 1984. Inspired by goings-on at the 8th Street Playhouse in New York the producers handed out to the audience as they entered ready-made packets of confetti,

matches and rice. These were intended as a helpful gesture to liven up the action during the wedding scenes, 'Over at the Frankenstein Place', and Frank's nuptials. 'I wish (expletive deleted),' says Paul Barnard now, 'we hadn't.'

Ecstatic acclaim greeted the new show. Basing themselves on the alternative libretto issued in the audience participation record album, people heckled the cast without mercy. Traditional shouts of 'asshole' and 'slut' greeted each entry of Brad and Janet. It was the Narrator, however, who from the start got the worst of it. The cast soon learned to judge the mood of the audience from its reaction to his first appearance. If he was allowed to make his opening remarks in silence it would probably be a dull evening. If, on the other hand, he were greeted with jeers and shouts of 'Is it true you're constipated?' and 'Is it true you're also gay?', then obviously interesting developments were to follow.

Audiences quickly learned to make full use of the confetti, matches and rice provided by an obliging management which soon stopped supplying them. Regulars brought along their own together with other props including bags of chips, salted and vinegared, to be thrown on stage as Dr Frank'n'Furter sings 'When the chips are down'. Ad-libbing was the only possible response. 'A bit limp, these,' he would say. 'Anybody got a harder one?' A Kit-Kat bar landed beside him.

References in the dialogue to hot dogs, mustard, toast and eggs evoke a shower of missiles. Golf balls have been thrown, and oranges spiked with nails and bars of soap. The Narrator was once knocked out by a bag of flour and has also been the target of a giant candle. One of the musicians suffered grave damage when a packet of peas sped through the air and hit him behind the ear. So much rice and water inundated Malcolm Sircom's keyboard that he had to rig up a plastic cover to shield it. In the end the band withdrew for safety's sake behind the scenes.

EXUBERANT FANS DOING THE TIME WARP

The most dramatic incident occurred during the second half one evening when a miscreant in the gallery hurled a giant water bomb filled with tin tacks down on the stage. It exploded noisily and stopped the performance. Before the show could begin again the police had to intervene. These days the Narrator issues a preliminary warning. 'No objects must be thrown. No missiles, no water, nothing. Water could get into the lasers.' The audience boos and stirs restlessly. His voice loudens melodramatically. 'If necessary, we will stop the performance. As you know, here in Hanley, we mean it . . . ' Sometimes, at the urging of the local Fire Service, anxious about matches and candles, he adds: 'Remember Bradford.'

'I've never seen anything so filthy and disgusting in my life,' said an usherette when the company was at the Alexandra Theatre in Birmingham. 'Why do we have shows like this?' She looked round her at piles of rubbish littering the auditorium. Spectators had had to move out of their seats when water showered down on them from the balcony above. Despite the vigilance of private security officers who seized water pistols and bags of rice from members of the audience, enough had been smuggled in to create havoc. Discarded balloons choked the cisterns of lavatories and candle grease trickled down the backs of seats.

At the Birmingham Hippodrome, also the scene of a visitation from *The Rocky Horror Show*, people in the audience grabbed water extinguishers and drenched the place. Future appearances were covered by special plans. The army of Draculas, Frank'n'Furters, Columbias, Riff-Raffs and visions apparelled in black plastic bin-liners were closely inspected as they came in. The harvest of illicit objects confiscated included balloons, garden sprayers and a hockey-stick.

As the news of *The Rocky Horror Show* spread around the provincial circuit, theatre managers adopted a wary attitude. There are, throughout England, quite a few charming Georgian and Victorian theatres which have escaped the blight of what is euphemistically called 'development'. Their owners are keen to preserve and maintain these delightful buildings. What they heard of *Rocky* and its rampageous audiences did not reassure them. Reluctantly, perhaps, they would book the show for a week just to see what happened. When they realized that each night they had full houses and box-office takings often far higher than any other attraction throughout the year, they made a return booking despite all the clearing up that had to be done after each performance. 'It is a very popular show,' they say. 'We have to give the public what it wants. We are criticized if the theatre is empty.' The Richmond Theatre in Surrey is a particularly fine example of Victorian architecture which needs considerable upkeep and cleaning. The management there have compromised by taking away some of the more obvious missiles audiences attempt to bring in with them. The result has been a varied collection of ironmongery and exotic underwear. The reward is extra twice-nightly performances which have had to be arranged to meet the unprecedented clamour for tickets.

The Theatre Royal Hanley's production of *The Rocky Horror Show* has been touring continuously since June 1984, and is booked solid for the next twelve months. By April 1986, it had drawn £1 million and long since covered its original investment of £20,000. Takings are now well on the way to approaching £2 million and there are no signs at the moment that the show's triumphant progress will ever stop. The management are always introducing new ideas. Rocky now makes his first appearance by stepping out of an enormous egg which trundles on stage. A great deal of money was recently invested in laser equipment, which, operated by a duo of permanent technicians, introduces kaleidoscopic effects when Riff-Raff switches the transit beam and launches the castle back through space to Transylvania. At present the management are toying with the notion, bearing in mind the problem posed by safety regulations, of giving Eddie a real motor bike to ride. There is the possibility of a rock video featuring songs from the score.

A CARTOONIST'S VIEW OF THE THEATRE DURING A PERFORMANCE

87

crush on Crush

After what will soon be three years of touring the cast is now more like a repertory company. New members are taken on, play their part, go away to fulfil other engagements, and then come back again. Auditions are usually held at the Pineapple Studios in Covent Garden. Such occasions are, as always, agonizing, not only for the hopefuls but also for the men in charge who hate turning people down. In a bare, mirrored, chilly room, the producers sit at tables littered with plastic cups and the debris of take-away meals. Outside, in a packed corridor, mills a crowd of up to 170 people chasing as few as six roles. One by one the candidates sing or dance in front of the panel. Some are extremely good. Others range from the mediocre to the pathetic. However talented the performers may be, there is still only a limited number of roles available. Judgements are delivered with seriousness and courtesy. 'Thank you, thank you very much' is the polite farewell which blandly hides a gamut of reactions which may run from the delighted to the appalled. It is just as well that *The Rocky Horror Show* is a Number One Tour for which membership of Equity is a prerequisite since otherwise the queues of aspirants would be swelled by hundreds, if not thousands, of would-be Frank'n'Furters and Columbias from audiences up and down the land.

As in all repertory companies, no one receives star billing. The names of individual performers are not even listed in the souvenir programmes. The play's the thing, so far as *The Rocky Horror Show* is concerned, and one could even argue that the audience is the star. There have, to date, been six Dr Frank'n'Furters. One of them was Dave Dale who had earlier distinguished himself as a drag queen stripper in the television serial *EastEnders*. Others were Bobby Bannerman and Cameron Stuart. Jeffrey Longmore, a product of Oldham, used to sing at Sadlers' Wells before playing a reporter in *The Free George Jackson Campaign* and taking parts in the TV soaps *Brookside* and *Coronation Street*.

The fourth Dr Frank was Bobby Crush.

◄ BOBBY CRUSH AS DR FRANK

When a cherubic eighteen-year-old he became known as the Charlie Charm of *Opportunity Knocks*, that venerable talent competition for amateurs in which he made no less than six winning appearances. That was fourteen years ago, since when he has figured in Royal charity shows and played the Palladium. He also won the Variety Club award as Best New Artiste.

After a decade or more of wooing the motherly instinct in his audiences he thought

JONATHAN KILEY AS DR FRANK ▲

it was time for something different. He scarcely expected to be offered *The Rocky Horror Show*. The producer, Paul Barnard, advised him to see it before deciding. He did, three times, and after the initial shock agreed to play Dr Frank-n-Furter.

Dr Frank, at the time of writing, is Jonathan Kiley who plays the part with demonic energy. A veteran from no less than six productions of *Godspell*, he has also mixed Shakespeare with Gilbert and Sullivan. On tour in Britain and North America he played *Elvis – The Musical*. Elsewhere he was a puckish Snoopy (*You're A Good Man, Charlie Brown*) and a combative Rooster (*Annie*).

DAVE DALE AS DR FRANK ▶

chunky pecs

One of the most statuesque of all Rockys is David Ian. Since leaving school he has been a professional pop singer with various groups and entered the BBC's *Song for Europe* in 1984 and 1986. On the second occasion he took his own band 'Jump' which has just released a new single. Many letters are sent him by fans ardent for unwashed pairs of the fishnet stockings he displays to spectacular advantage in the finale of *The Rocky Horror Show*.

Quite by chance his fellow player Julie Faye sang with him in 'Jump' during the Eurovision Song Contest. She is Columbia, a pert dancer who once understudied Su Pollard in the tour of *Hi-De-Hi*. She sings as neatly as she dances and has travelled Europe and the Middle East with various cabaret shows. She brings to Columbia a wistful sauciness that is immediately appealing.

DAVID IAN AS
ROCKY

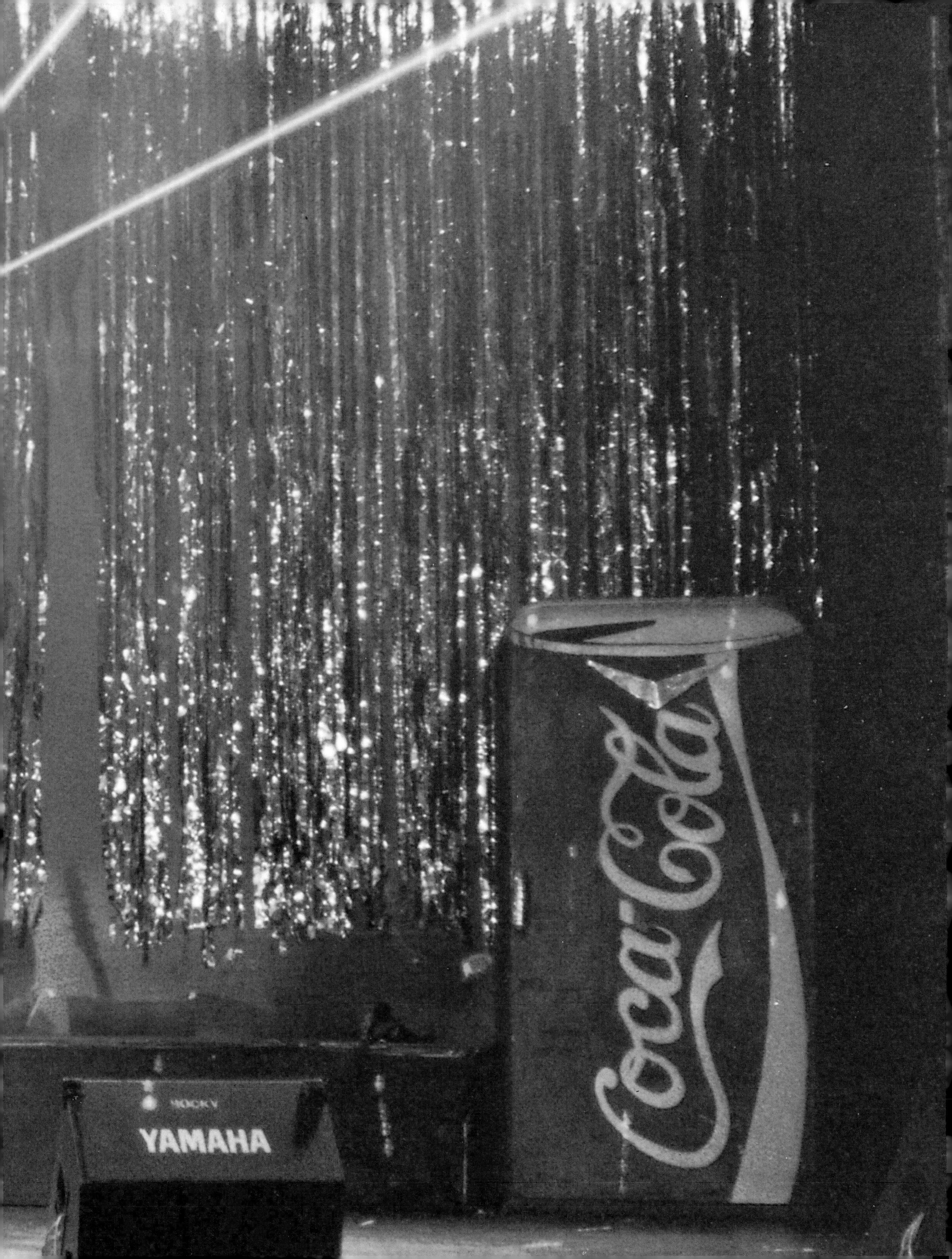
YAMAHA
Coca-Cola

sex change

*T*he Rocky Horror Show has altered many lives. It has brought stardom to actors and actresses and, behind the scenes, has enriched many people who are unknown to the public. Thousands of fans have had their existence transformed by it. One person, indeed, has actually changed sex on the way.

This is Kinny Gardner who has played Riff-Raff on tour — a Riff-Raff with black hair, kiss-curl, arching eyebrows and sharp questing nose. Back in the 1970s when he was a seventeen-year-old boy he joined the cast of the original London production. He took over the part of Columbia which had been played up to then by Little Nell. After that he toured with the Kaboodle Theatre Exchange and worked as co-artistic director of the Krazy Kat Theatre Company. His gift for the sinister was flamboyantly displayed as Rossignol in *Marat/Sade* and as the ambiguous Master of Ceremonies in *Cabaret*. Later on he became a girl again as Jenny in *The Threepenny Opera*. His playing of Riff-Raff is not at all like Richard O'Brien's. 'I don't believe in copying other people,' he explains. 'I've been in the business for fourteen years and I get employed for what I do — so my version of Riff-Raff is very different from the one the writer Richard O'Brien made familiar in the film. But then, he was first portrayed as a Bela Lugosi figure, so there have been changes before.'

The one unchanging figure in *The Rocky Horror Show* is that of Brad Majors, a character, you feel, whom neither earthquakes nor the satanic mischief of Dr Frank'n'Furter could ever succeed in denting. Chris Marlowe gives to Brad a quizzical perplexity that survives all the shocks and indignities piled upon him. Once a hairdresser, trained for the stage at Bristol University, he has, like the rest of the cast, a solid background of musicals which include *Joseph and the Amazing Technicolor Dreamcoat* (also toured by the Theatre Royal Hanley), *Jesus Christ Superstar*, *The Boy Friend* and *A Funny Thing Happened on the Way to the Forum*.

His fiancee Janet Weiss, whose name occasions ribaldry in the audience, is incarnated by the natural blonde hair and dark brown eyes of Jayne Moore. She emerged from the Guildford School of Acting and Dance to tour with Scandinavian World Cruises and then to appear in pantomime. Her wide vocal range, which has been admired in operetta like *The Pirates of Penzance*, enables her to endow 'Touch-a-touch-a-touch-a-touch me' with a ring of innocence that is not entirely satirical. She also charms many an aspiring man on the beat through the medium of various police training films she has made.

The character who tries, manfully, to hold the show together is the Narrator. He is at once derided and beloved of the audience, a figure of authority and a scapegoat. For some time now he has been played by Peter Thorne who trained for the stage in Cardiff. After working as assistant stage manager at the Swansea Grand he was invited to take over a part in the thriller *A Touch of Fear*, since when he has been in the lucky position of never having had to audition for a role.

The Narrator's classically greying hair, bow tie and elegant velvet jacket make him, Peter thinks, an Establishment figure apparently dedicated to discipline and law and order. In many respects he is a pivotal character since without him and what he represents *The Rocky Horror Show* would lack a target for its mockery. The Narrator provides an excuse to stand convention on its head. As the unforgiving hail of rice and water and soggy toast sloshes on stage he rides the whirlwind, only to capitulate at the end when he, too, throws in his lot with the others and comes on at the finale wearing suspender belt and garters.

JULIA HOWSON (JANET) AND CHRISTOPHER MALCOLM (BRAD)

random fandom fandom

The following acquired over the years by *The Rocky Horror Show* is sometimes described as a cult. If used in the modern sense, with implications of a small clique, it is not quite the proper word to define an army of many thousands. The Hanley production can fill the 3000 seats of the Edinburgh Playhouse just as easily as it can pack the 900-plus capacity of Bath Theatre Royal. A week at Leeds is capable of attracting 15,000 people. In Aberdeen, Glasgow, Manchester and Bristol it plays to thousands more. If one studies the box-office figures and allows for return visits by the audience and repeat bookings, it is possible, on the most conservative basis, to estimate the number of fans at 250,000. Only then can the word cult be used in its older sense of devotion to an object paid by a body of adherents.

The Rocky Horror Show is accompanied everywhere by what the management has learned to call 'the travelling audience'. This is made up of groups, often all girls, who, rigged up in Space Age millinery, hire special coaches to take them to performances. En route they do the 'Time Warp' as their conveyance speeds along the motorway. It's an outing for them and no more significant in Freudian terms than the char-a-banc trips their grandparents laid on to Southend or Blackpool for a day of whelks and kiss-me-quick hats. They see it as a chance to dress up, 'to take you out of yourself'. At Wimbledon recently two special trains were chartered to bring people from London for the show. Other fans are pilgrims who wander from Hastings to Manchester, from Brighton to Aberdeen in pursuit of Rocky.

England can offer nothing like the systematically organized American fan club inspired by the film. Instead, faithful to ideals of English pragmaticism, there exist a few loosely knit groups which propagate the gospel with amiable informality. 'The Denton Convention' at West Molesey, Surrey, recently put on a Rocky Horror/Shock Treatment weekend. The three committee members, while enjoying *The Rocky Horror Show*, are not involved in the talk-back rituals although they take a benevolent interest in other fans. The event was scheduled, explains Donna Lauchlan, 'because there has never been a *Rocky Horror* Convention here before and the majority of potential attenders appear to be outside "mainstream" media science fiction/ Star Trek fandom which we are more accustomed to . . . ' All proceeds went to the Save The Children Fund.

The 'Fat Club' of Aberdeen encourages audience participation by circulating cue sheets in theatres and leading the responses. In Glasgow a dedicated band are present to 'introduce' the film when it is run at local cinemas and to greet the touring company wherever it appears within a 100-mile radius. Often they help out at the souvenir stall.

Letters continue to pour in at the Hanley Theatre Royal. People who have been following the show ever since it went on tour three years back know all the dialogue and songs as well as individual performers. Any changes in the cast or decor are submitted to expert analysis. The merits of the 'Dave Dale' cast are assessed in relation to the 'Bobby Crush', the 'Cameron Stuart', the 'Bobby Bannerman', the 'Jeffrey Longmore' and the 'Jonathan Kiley'. Some of the changes are hailed as 'excellent' and others allowed 'to show promise'. Make-up is critically analysed and costume searchingly examined. The departure of a favourite actor is lamented and the 'business' he introduced sadly missed. New arrivals among the cast are put on probation and warned to keep up standards set by performers who now belong to the lore and legend of the show. Junior players who have been promoted to main roles are congratulated but, at the same time, are exhorted to remember the excellence of those who have gone before. Why, continue the writers of these letters, does not 'X' sing clearly or 'Z' wear a more becoming wig? How does it come about, they protest, that 'Y' should be given a role 'when so many actors are unemployed'? They speak more in sorrow than in anger for they are zealous above all to preserve the quality of what they know as 'Richard O'Brien's masterpiece'.

ANNOUNCEMENT OF THE ROCKY HORROR/ SHOCK TREATMENT WEEKEND ►

A ROCKY HORROR Shock Treatment WEEKEND

The Denton Convention

TO BE HELD 13/14 SEPTEMBER 1986

AT THE SHEPPERTON MOAT HOUSE HOTEL (MIDDX)

REGISTRATION RATES: *(weekend/per person)*

£8·00 UNTIL 2nd JANUARY '86

£10·00 UNTIL 2nd JULY '86

£12·00 THEREAFTER

PROCEEDS TO THE SAVE THE CHILDREN FUND.

wonderful! brilliant! astonishing!

Others are less critical. 'Dear Mr Barnard', or 'Dear Paul', begins a typical letter which goes on to speak of 'the wonderful night out that I had last Saturday when I saw *The Rocky Horror Show*. I thought it was wonderful — the cast were brilliant and the scenery was fantastic (particularly the lasers) and the atmosphere created by the audience was astonishing. I didn't mind one bit when I was covered in rice, playing cards, confetti, and showered in water, the audience was wonderful. The night out was well worth the £4 I paid for my ticket and it was great value for money.' For the writers of letters like this, and there are many of them, *The Rocky Horror Show* has been a revelation. They cannot wait to see it again and the 'travelling audience' gains still more recruits.

Often a note of pathos is struck, especially when the *Rocky* virus bites deep. A girl from one of the big Northern towns happened to see the film and became a convert. Soon afterwards she saw the stage production and was overwhelmed. Dave Dale played Dr Frank'n'Furter and 'in fact the whole cast were brilliant. Watching them gave me so much energy, I could have stayed at the theatre all night dancing away but unfortunately it was all over much too quickly and the curtain fell and the theatre emptied. But I was hooked by then. I was dying to go backstage to meet them and just see how it all works but of course I couldn't so it was back home. I didn't sleep a wink that night. I relived the show a dozen times in my mind as I could remember every movement.' Until then she had been a student on a course learning to type. *The Rocky Horror Show* became her Epiphany, her road to Damascus, and she left the course because 'I knew what I wanted to do and it didn't involve typing.'

Next day she felt she had to see the show again. It was a Saturday, the last performance of the week, and all seats were sold. She did not give in easily, and after eloquent pleading at the box-office was able to charm a pair of tickets out of the staff. With her mother she sat in the back row, and although she had been at the front on the previous night, there was 'still the same electrifying atmosphere'. She would, she confessed, have sat anywhere just to be in the

theatre. At the end she came away once more 'in another world'.

When, next week, the show moved to another town, she was there doing the 'Time Warp' on cue and feeling a part of it all. Afterwards she and a friend went into the bar for a drink and found some of the cast. Pleasantries were exchanged and autographs solicited. 'We had a quick chat to all of them but then we had to go. I longed to be able to go with them, any part would have done, absolutely anything. But of course this was an impossible dream.'

On the next occasion when *The Rocky Horror Show* visited a neighbouring town she booked three nights in succession and took her parents along to one of them. Curiosity assailed her brother who was impelled to reserve a seat for himself as well. During weeks of agonized waiting she and her girl friend plundered the shops for fishnet stockings, basques and suspender belts. While they tried them on secretly and studied the effect in mirrors they were overcome with laughter at the thought of her brother's reaction. The great night came and they appeared in all their punkish splendour. The brother nearly fainted with surprise 'but my Mum and Dad loved it'. They loved the show, too, and so did her brother who soon recovered from the shock and was anxious to book seats for another performance.

Fan letters to the cast brought charming replies, although they did not succeed in appeasing the strange yearnings that moved her. The days became longer and her existence increasingly boring. It proved impossible to find a job and the vista of unemployment stretched blankly in front of her.

One night, in a deep depression, she saw from an advertisement that *The Rocky Horror Show* was visiting her local theatre again. Happiness broke out and seats were taken for three performances culminating in Saturday which was to be a family occasion with Mum, Dad and brother. When she saw that Bobby Crush of all people was to play Frank she could not imagine him in the part. Neither could her mother who, by then, was almost as word-perfect in the dialogue and lyrics as she herself. 'Oh well,' they said, 'at least give him a chance.' They could not, however, see the boyish charmer doing

much with the role. At the first night in the theatre they cringed when he made his entrance. Almost immediately he came over to them, took her hand and kissed her. The magic worked. They thought him terrific, even though she could not suppress an errant affection for Riff-Raff who, she decided after much thoughtful reappraisal, was her true favourite. There were drinks with the cast afterwards, autographs were garnered and everyone posed for a photograph.

After which the bubble dissolved and life returned to its monochrome routine coloured only by the letters, the pictures, the autographs, the souvenirs. She wrote:

> I don't mind telling you that we cried after the last show on Saturday. The thought of not seeing the show to us is so depressing. Our ambition is to be in the show but we know it will never come true. It is such a wonderful production and we would love to be part of it. I know this letter will go straight in the bin but please think about it. We don't expect a life of glamour and riches but we know it would be great fun. There are so many things I would like to ask you but I have taken up enough of your time already. Please say you'll be doing another tour soon and if you do ever get any parts you know who to think of. We'd be eternally grateful. If this is too much to ask, then how about a day with you all to see how things go on?

As Mr Micawber would have said, the canker was in the flower, the cup bitter to the brim and the worm at his work. But a spark of hope could be discerned. A hasty postscript added that *The Rocky Horror Show* was soon to make a return visit to the local theatre and that she had booked four nights. The names of the cast had not been announced, 'but whoever it is it will be as brilliant as ever'. Perhaps, after all, there will be a happy ending.

Letters such as these would provide rich material for the social scientists and psychologists who are deep in study of the *Rocky* phenomenon. Learned theories about 'subcult performance-oriented entertainment' are connected with the revolt against passivity. Transexual behaviour and cross-dressing are seen as springing from fear of failure and economic insecurity. Androgyny is postulated as a way of overcoming sexual confusion because it offers more choice and the opportunity to experiment. *Rocky*, say the theorists, helps alienated youth to free itself from class restrictions and sexual taboos and

to enter a fantasy world of hedonistic pleasure. Theses abound in the attempt to explain *The Rocky Horror Show* and its grip on audiences. A-level students have even written dissertations on the subject and have mused, from the viewpoint of seventeen-year-olds, on 'the fashions of the mid-1970s' which for them are a part of the ancient world, at one with Nineveh and Tyre. Their elucubrations have been received with startled interest by examining boards.

Meanwhile the fun goes on. At Bath Theatre Royal, where *The Rocky Horror Show* followed Monteverdi's *L'Incoronazione di Poppea*, the most outrageously dressed member of the audience received a prize of champagne from Dr Frank'n'Furter. In Bradford, at the Alhambra Theatre, the bottle of champagne went to Billy Rankin of Spring Valley Walk, Bramley. He whisked on stage in a froth of taffeta and tulle as Frankenstein's bride, and, a subtle homage to the Narrator, twirled between his fingers an elegant cigarette-holder.

AUDIENCE LOOK-ALIKES FRANK AND MAGENTA

Rocky on the road

Despite scenes of near-riot and the clearing up necessary afterwards theatre managers continue to welcome *The Rocky Horror Show* as it travels England crisscrossing the motorways and doubling back on its tracks, one week in Leamington, the next in Halifax, the one after that in Richmond. Manchester, Scarborough, Dundee and Portsmouth whirl by in a blur of fishnets and lasers. Only in Blackpool, when the famous lights are switched on, does it come up against real competition.

A van and a roomy pantechnicon ferry the elaborate lighting and amplifying equipment and scenery from town to town. Transport is a large item in the weekly budget at £1000, though not so high as the figure for salaries which is over five times this. Next, in order of size, come the royalties that have to be paid under complicated agreements governing the show. With Oxford generating £31,000 of revenue, Birmingham £34,000 and Leeds £38,000, there is enough left over to satisfy the requirements of Value Added Tax and the Commissioners of Her Majesty's Inland Revenue.

The atmosphere backstage is relaxed and light-hearted. Team-spirit is warm and the sense of belonging to a successful show keeps morale at a very high level. Ivor Novello, who loved going on tour, used to say it was like having a first night every week with all the excitement and novelty repeated each Monday. Even the too-zealous fans who trespass behind the scenes and gate-crash

LINE-UP OF A THEATRE ROYAL
HANLEY CAST

dressing rooms are escorted out with kindly tolerance. If *The Rocky Horror Show* company were in the Navy, which they most definitely are not, you would describe them with the traditional phrase 'a happy ship'.

The Hanley Theatre Royal would like to see *The Rocky Horror Show* in the West End as a follow-up to its other triumphs there, *Cabaret* and *The Hobbit*. This, however, is impossible under the terms of its contract. When *Rocky* came to the Town and Country Club at Tottenham and grossed £37,000 in a

week there were uneasy murmurs. 'We got our knuckles rapped over that one,' says Paul Barnard. 'The rights holders said it counted as the West End — and we're not allowed in there.'

Richard O'Brien, who started it all, thinks the touring version is too broad, and for that reason he does not care to see it in the West End. 'There's no horror, no danger,' he opines. 'The *threat* of sexuality is there in the original but it is a play written out of repression. Frank has his way with everyone but no one else does, they're under his control. It's a very repressed little set-up. Which is why it does well in repressed societies. Like Australia.' Nonetheless, at Christmas he sent a crate of champagne to the cast.

Disapproving critics have sometimes referred to the Hanley show as a pubescent panto. It is true that people who saw the 1973 original would now find it mightily changed. There are good reasons for this. The cast appearing in The Theatre Upstairs production did not have to project into the wide open spaces of England's biggest theatres. They did not have to make themselves clearly visible at the back of the vast Liverpool

... Rocky on the road

Empire with its 2,300 seats, and neither were they obliged to pitch their voices so that they carried to the furthermost reach of the gallery at the Manchester Palace. The *Rocky Horror Show* now plays regularly to numbers up to forty times the audience that first witnessed it at The Theatre Upstairs. Inevitably actions need to be magnified and grimaces exaggerated.

To judge by the 1973 cast recording the music is performed at much the same rate. Except for an oddly somnolent 'Time Warp' on the record, tempi are identical and the beat comes over with pulsing urgency. It is the circumstances which have changed completely. The original cast faced an audience of West End sophisticates. The touring production has to confront assemblies of high-spirited young people out for a good time and bristling with an armoury of missiles. To the normal abilities of acting, dancing and singing must be added quickness of foot to dodge the bigger objects that are thrown and a politician's gift for dealing with hecklers.

A comparison between the film of *The Rocky Horror Show* and the current stage production reveals the gulf that will always shut off the cinema from live entertainment. The film itself, apart from preserving the excellent performances of many original cast members, is abundantly witty and imaginative. It is played with exhilarating verve and directed with brilliance. The very fact, though, of its being imprisoned for ever on film means that it remains frozen and immutable. The players have done their bit and departed. There is nothing to add. This is underlined by the fans' habit of dancing among themselves while the film is shown unheeded. The stage production, however, is a living thing that grows and develops in sympathy with those who watch it. Every performance is unique and emerges from a happy conspiracy between the players and the audience. Whatever the sociological implications of *The Rocky Horror Show*, regardless of the meanings thoughtful commentators have read into the text, it gloriously affirms a tradition which is many centuries old: the supremacy of live theatre.

FROM THE THEATRE ROYAL HANLEY PRODUCTION

cast lists

The Theatre Upstairs, Royal Court Theatre, London SW3. Produced by Michael White. Previewed 16 and 18 June 1973. Opened 19 June for a limited season. Opened at the Classic, Chelsea, 14 August 1973. Transferred to the King's Road Classic, 3 November 1973. Transferred to the Comedy Theatre, 6 April 1979. Run of 2,960 performances ended 13 September 1980.

Cast (names of players who succeeded original actors and actresses given in brackets):

Usherette/Magenta
Patricia QUINN (Angela Bruce, Leueen Willoughby, Bryan Joan Elliot, Pippa Hardman, Joanna Lloyd, Kathryn Drew, Leni Harper and others).

Janet Weiss
Julie COVINGTON (Belinda Sinclair, Anne-Louise Wakefield, Ellie Smith, Pippa Hardman, Tracey Ullman and others).

Brad Majors
Christopher MALCOLM (James Warwick, Hayward Morse, Frederick Marks, Steve Devereaux and others).

Narrator
Jonathan ADAMS (Tom Chatto, Bob Hornery, Jeffrey Chiswick, George Little and others).

Riff-Raff
Richard O'BRIEN (Robert Longden, Neil McCaul, Perry Bedden, David Glyn Rogers and others).

Columbia
Little NELL (Anna Nygh, Linda Dobell, Joanna Lloyd, Kinny Gardner, Melanie Wallis, Bryan Joan Elliot and others).

Dr Frank'n'Furter
Tim CURRY (Philip Sayer, Peter Blake, Robert Longden, Ziggy Byfield, Shaughan Seymour, Neil McCaul, Daniel Abineri and others).

Rocky Horror
Rayner BOURTON (Ben Bazell, Nigel Bowden, Miles Fothergill, Jeremy Gittins and others).

Eddie/Dr Scott
Paddy O'HAGAN (Ziggy Byfield, Shaughan Seymour, Nick Llewellyn, Gary Olsen and others).

Also appearing:
Jean McArthur, James Supervia, Lewis Barber, Tim Earle, David Glyn Rogers, Diane Robillard, Paul Woods, Harriet Arkwright, Raymond Sawyer, Paul Woodson, Colen Marsh, Eric Nordell, Kay Parkes, Roger Tebb, Tessa Wood, Jane Hayward, Gary Martin, Julie Ashton and others.

Director:
Jim Sharman.

Musical Director and Arranger
Richard (Ritz) Hartley (piano, organ, synthesizer); with Ian Blair (electric/ acoustic guitar), Dave Channing (alto/ tenor sax, bass guitar), Martin Fitzgibbon (drums).

Scene Designer:
Brian Thomson.

Costume Designer:
Sue Blane.

Assistant Costume Designer:
Colin MacNeil.

Lighting:
Gerry Jenkinson.

Lighting Operator:
Peter Hunt.

Stage Manager:
Chris Peachment.

Assistant Stage Managers:
Alkis Kritikos, Marion Kernahan.

New York stage production

Belasco Theatre, New York. Produced by Lou Adler. 10 March 1975. Run of 45 performances ended 6 April 1975.

The Belasco
Popcorn Girl (Trixie) Jamie DONNELLY
Janet Abigail HANESS
Brad Bill MILLER
Narrator William NEWMAN
Riff-Raff Ritz O'BRIEN
Columbia Boni ENTEN
Magenta Jamie DONNELLY
Frank Tim CURRY
Rocky Kim MILFORD
Eddie MEATLOAF
Dr Scott MEATLOAF
Director: Jim Sharman
Scene Designer: Brian Thomson
Costume Designer: Sue Blane.

film version

Twentieth-Century Fox. Made in Great Britain on location at Oakley Court and at Bray Studios: post-production at EMI Studios, Elstree. A Michael White/Lou Adler production. 1975.

Magenta/Lips Patricia QUINN

Janet Susan SARANDON

Brad Barry BOSTWICK

Narrator/Criminologist Charles GRAY

Riff-Raff Richard O'BRIEN

Columbia Little NELL

Dr Frank'n'Furter Tim CURRY

Rocky Peter HINWOOD

Eddie MEATLOAF

Dr Everett Scott Jonathan ADAMS

Bridesmaid Koo STARK

Ralph Hapschatt Jeremy NEWSON

Betty Munroe Hilary LABOW

Transylvanians Christopher BIGGINS, Gayle BROWN, Ishaq BUX, Stephen CALCUTT, Hugh CECIL, Imogen CLAIRE, Rufus COLLINS, Sadie CORRIE, Tony COWAN, Fran FULLENWIDER, Lindsay INGRAM, Peggy LEDGER, Annabel LEVENTON, Anthony MILNER, Pamela OBERMEYER, Tony THEN, Kimi WONG, Henry WOOLF.

From the play *The Rocky Horror Show*, book, music and lyrics by Richard O'Brien. Screenplay: Richard O'Brien and Jim Sharman.

Producer: Michael White.

Director: Jim Sharman.

Cinematography: Peter Suschitzky.

Editor: Graeme Clifford.

Scene designer: Brian Thomson.

Costume designer: Sue Blane.

Choreography: David Toguri.

Musical Director: Richard Hartley.

Running time: 100 minutes.

Theatre Royal Hanley touring production

Producer: Paul Barnard, Charles Deacon.

Executive Producer: John Farrow.

Production Assistant: Angela Taprogge.

Director: Vivyan Ellacott.

Choreography: Lorraine Porter.

Musical Director: Malcolm Sircom (keyboards), with Ken Newton (drums), Cyril Newton (bass), Tony Smith (guitar), Alan Miller (saxophone).

Lighting: Andrew Stone.

Costumes: Nigel Ellacott.

Company Manager: Peter Thorne.

Laser: Laserplay Ltd.

Scenery: Ian Wilson.

First performance: Theatre Royal, Hanley, Stoke-on-Trent, 7 June 1984, since when it has toured continuously and played all over England.

The cast varies from time to time. Players of Dr Frank'n'Furter so far include Jonathan Kiley, Bobby Crush, Jeffrey Longmore, Bobby Bannerman, Dave Dale and Cameron Stuart. The current Brad Majors is Christopher Marlowe; Janet has been played by Julia Howson and Jayne Moore; Riff-Raff by Kinny Gardner and Paul Critchlow, and Rocky Horror by Jean-Paul Orr and David Ian. The Usherette and Magenta have been doubled by Adeen Fogle and Daliah Wood. Columbia has been played by Julie Faye and Lorinda King; Eddie by Andrew Ryan and Marc Seymour; Dr Scott by Mark Turnbull and Patrick French; The Narrator by John North and Peter Thorne.

The tour continues with many return visits to theatres already played in addition to plans for an overseas tour.

discography

Original London Cast
LP UA UKAL 1006. 1973, 1986

Original Australian Cast
LP Festival L35231. 1974

Original Los Angeles Cast
SP ODE SP77026. 1974

Original Mexican Cast
LP.Orfeon 13.2277. 1978

Original New Zealand Cast
LP Stetson Records LPSRLP6. 1979

Original West German Cast
LP Ariola 202.146.315. 1980

Australian Revival Cast
EP. Festival L20009. 1981

British Film Soundtrack
LP.Ode 78332, OPD91653. 1975

British Film Soundtrack
Audience Participation Album (2 records),
Ode 1983

The Rocky Horror Disco Show
LP. Vocal/ Instrumental. ZYX Records 5299

acknowledgements

My thanks to:

RICHARD O'BRIEN
alias Riff-Raff, without whom there would have been no subject for this book, and with whom, thanks to the documentation and hospitality which he dispensed in equally generous measure, the author was enabled to write it;

JONATHAN ADAMS
alias the Narrator and Dr Scott;

RAYNER BOURTON
alias Rocky, a creation;

CHARLES GREY
alias the Narrator;

SUSAN HILL
who refused to be floored;

SAL PIRO
animator of the American Fan Club;

LYNDA SAUNDERS
wizard of the word processor;

THE THEATRE ROYAL HANLEY
PLC – Charles DEACON, Chairman; John E. JONES, Director and Secretary; John FARROW, Executive Producer; Peter THORNE, Actor and Manager; Trish SEETO, Public Relations Officer;

MICHAEL WHITE
Producer of the 1973 stage show and of the film.

The following organizations were also very helpful:
Barry Stacey Productions Ltd; The British Film Institute; Cameron Hayward & Co. Ltd; Chatto & Linnit Ltd; London Management Ltd. (Richard Grenville).

First published in Great Britain in October 1987 by Sidgwick & Jackson Limited

First reprint December 1987

Copyright © 1987 by James Harding
Designed by Roger Walker Design

Photographs were supplied or are reproduced by kind permission of the following:
Colorific! 4, 8, 13, 35, 78-9, 80-1, 86, 92, 97, 99, 100 and all colour photographs.
Donald Cooper 6-7, 9, 11, 26, 50, 53, 58-9, 70, 71, 76
Johnny Rozsa, 16, 17
Warner Pathe 20
James Harding 27, 45, 84-5
Jonathan Adams 51
Theatre Royal, Hanley 84-5, 88, 89, 90-1, 93, 98

ISBN 0–283–99388–X

Typeset by Falcon Graphic Art Ltd, Wallington, Surrey
Printed and bound in Great Britain by Butler & Tanner Ltd, Frome and London for Sidgwick & Jackson Limited
1 Tavistock Chambers, Bloomsbury Way London WC1A 2SG